WHEN SILENCE IS GOLDEN

WOW LIFE
PUBLISHING

Printed in the United States of America

Paper back ISBN 978-1-957287-12-6
Kindle: ISBN: 978-1-957287-20-1

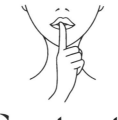

Contents

Dedication

This book is dedicated to two incredibly important figures in my life.

Firstly, to my heavenly Father, the true Master of golden silence who has always been by my side. In my times of grief and loss, through Your silent presence, I felt Your comforting and loving nature, and I am deeply grateful.

Secondly, to my beloved grandmother, Justina Sealys, affectionately known as Acha. You are the one who cut my umbilical cord, but you have also been a constant presence since the day I entered this world. You witnessed my first steps, heard my first words, and imparted invaluable life lessons that have guided me. Acha, you are my hero. It was an incredible joy for you to witness the birth of my first book and grace the book signing with your presence. Mumo, I love you dearly.

To my family, especially my daughter, Latisha Sealys, thank you for your unwavering love and support. May the memories of our departed loved ones forever reside in our hearts.

Foreword

Life eventually comes to an end—this is everyone's destiny, and it is there for all of us to see. Often, we believe we understand life, how to live it, and how to love others because we witness their lives unfolding before our eyes. However, it is during the most despairing and sorrowful times of a grief-stricken person that we truly come to understand pain, suffering, and loss.

The truth is many people do not understand life, love, death, and grief. They see but do not see; they listen but do not hear and so they consistently fail others during periods of grief. There is often much misunderstanding surrounding life, love, death, and grief.

Understanding a grieving person can be challenging because death encompasses an unspoken emotional pain that persists during and after the loss of a loved one, sometimes for a long time thereafter. Frequently, people respond to this emotional pain based on their own perceptions, past experiences, learned societal patterns, and even denial. They fail to truly listen and only understand what they already know. Sadly, this is often because they do not know how to react, what to say, or even how to say it. A grieving person has difficulty coping with the loss and finding the strength to appreciate life without their loved one. So, who will teach people how to cope with or communicate effectively with someone drowning in grief?

Jermila Sealys has lived through life's darkest moments, having faced consecutive losses of her dearest and most loved ones. Through her own journey, she uncovers the untold truth of insensitive communication with someone who is emotionally grieving.

When Silence is Golden serves as a guide to help people cope with those who are grieving. The narratives and experiences shared in this book aim to coach readers on what the grieving person is going through, how to handle them, the most appropriate way to act toward them, and what to say or avoid saying.

This book is purposeful, versatile, and recommended for anyone, regardless of their background. Death and loss are universal experiences that affect us all.

It has been a pleasure knowing Jermila Sealys since 2008 in a friendship that has gone from mere acquaintances to a family bond. I appreciate her contributions and her honesty in addressing this universal struggle. Despite the pain she has experienced, she has found the words to express a common perception of those who grieve and teach others how to see what is actually happening to a grieving person, hear the grieving person, as well as support and attend to the needs of a grieving person.

Allison Hermia Tench
Associate Attorney
O'Neal Webster

Prologue

I can vividly recall that fateful day when my beloved uncle, Ezekiel, passed away, even though I was just a 10-year-old child at the time. That was my first encounter with the cold hand of sudden death. My day unfolded like any ordinary school day, with my brother, cousins, and me getting ready for school from 9 a.m. to 3 p.m. The sun painted a warm glow over the world, and the sky displayed a mesmerizing canvas of clear blue adorned with fluffy cotton-white clouds.

I had seen my uncle earlier that day. It was a workday for him. Perhaps we exchanged a few words in passing, saying the usual "Good morning, Uncle." As far as I knew, he was in perfect health. Little did I know that would be my last time seeing him. His passing happened so quickly that I didn't even know what happened. All I could remember were a few screams from the adults in the family. I couldn't recall my mother or anyone else mentioning any signs of illness or discomfort. But it was an unremarkable day, just like any other.

As the days that followed unfolded, I started hearing a word utterly foreign to my young ears: "postmortem." The sound of it sent chills down my spine. It was a word that lingered in the air, unspoken yet profoundly present, as my family struggled with the sudden departure of Uncle Ezekiel.

To this day, I remain uncertain about the circumstances surrounding his untimely passing. The mysteries of that day continue to haunt me, a persistent puzzle residing in the depths of my memory. It stands as a heartbreaking reminder that life can take unexpected and sudden turns. Even on the sunniest of days, shadows can descend, and the world can change in an instant. As children, we are shielded from the harsh truths of mortality. But as we grow older, we come to understand the weight carried by words like "postmortem" and the delicate nature of life itself.

In every family, there's that one person who is universally adored, and in our family, Uncle Ezekiel was that cherished figure. He held a special place in our hearts, and his memory remains etched in our minds. I can still recall those precious moments before his sudden passing.

Uncle Ezekiel worked at JQ Charles supermarket in Vieux-Fort, and his daily routine included a heartwarming tradition. After a long day at work, he would come bearing gifts for each one of us: lollipops, popcorn, cheese sticks, and an abundance of other treats. But the fun part was that these treats were never simply handed over; we had to earn them through some of the craziest and most enjoyable challenges he put together.

One of Uncle Ezekiel's passions was photography, and he had an instant camera that required vigorous shaking until the image appeared. He captured every moment, from our silliest antics to our proudest achievements—birthdays, first days of school, and my first Communion. Those photographs now reside in my grandmother's cherished photo album, reminding us of the joy we experienced together.

Uncle Ezekiel's presence was so vital to our daily lives that coming home from school without him around was a sheer contrast. Our family home felt different, although we were too young to truly grasp the concept of death and the profound impact it would have on us.

One particular afternoon during the time of my uncle's passing, as my cousins and I approached our home, we sensed an unusual atmosphere. Laughter and voices resounded from afar, some of them unfamiliar to our young ears. It was a gathering, a congregation of sorts, with both familiar faces from our community and some we scarcely knew. Among them were distant family members who usually visited for holidays and special family occasions.

Surveying the yard, it was evident that people had come together, performing various tasks—cooking, chopping wood, sweeping, fetching water, and more. The community had united to support our grieving family, and what struck me most was the proximity of sadness and joy. The adults chatted and shared light-hearted moments, even in the face of tragedy, undertaking their tasks with unwavering dedication and love. Their actions spoke volumes about their compassion for our family during this sudden loss.

The ladies kindly asked us to change out of our school uniforms and made sure we were fed. It seemed as if the house was constantly filled with people, and they remained by our side, day and night. It felt as if they worked in shifts, with one group leaving in the morning and another arriving in the evening. For nine days, we were excused from school until after the burial. I cherished those nights when people took turns telling stories, singing folk songs, and playing instruments like bamboo drums. I even learned to play dominoes and cards during those unforgettable evenings.

While it was a time of mourning, it was also a period filled with laughter. I can't recall anyone bombarding us with questions; instead, they offered their presence and support. They anticipated our needs and acted selflessly. Food was always available, and everyday tasks were carried out with love and care. Those moments were a testament to the power of silent solidarity.

Fast forward to this era of the internet and smartphones, and things have changed significantly within our generation. People often offer advice or ask probing questions quickly instead of simply being present. They may say, "I can feel your pain" or "I know how you're feeling" without truly understanding the depth of grief. Well-intentioned words can often inadvertently cause more harm than good.

I remember, a few days after my mother's passing, someone suggested that it might have been a spiritual attack on my family. In my vulnerable state, I allowed myself to believe it, searching for someone or something to blame for my mother's death. Looking back, I realise that this redirected my grief into unproductive channels as I worried about whether it was true or not. In my anger and confusion, I even questioned God's role in our family's suffering.

Emotions during the initial stages of grief can be overwhelming, and words spoken at that time need to be gentle and thoughtful. Those who are grieving often hear only what they choose to hear, and negative sentiments can easily take root. It's like selective hearing, where the mind fixates on the most damaging interpretations.

We will all experience grief at some point in our lives, and there is a noticeable lack of guidance and support on how to interact with someone who is grieving. Some things are better left unsaid, and some words are a soothing balm to a wounded soul. Finding the right words can be a delicate art, and there's no handbook or instruction manual. In such moments, we should strive for compassion and empathy, offering our presence, rather than well-intentioned but potentially hurtful advice.

Navigating the delicate task of supporting our family and friends during their most challenging moments can leave us feeling at a loss for words. In times of grief, finding the right thing to say can be difficult. We often feel compelled to offer comfort, even when words seem insufficient. Unfortunately, in our attempt to console, our words can inadvertently hurt, cutting through the heart like a merciless sword and inflicting pain without visible wounds or bleeding.

It is precisely for these reasons that I invite you to join me on a journey through the pages of this book. I aim to guide not only what to say but also how to say it when a loved one is struggling with the intense and complex emotions that come with grief. In this unwelcome season of their lives, I hope to help them navigate the terrain of empathy and support, offering solace and understanding when it is most needed.

About the Book

Let's face it; when those around us are grieving, we don't always know what to say. In times like these, we often rely on everyday sayings such as "I am sorry for your loss," "I know how you feel," or "I can feel your pain." But do these words truly provide comfort?

This book is a guide to help you learn how to support those who are grieving and how to communicate empathetically with them, often without using words. It will teach you how to consider your words before offering advice or making comments that you believe are comforting but may be received differently by the person who is grieving.

So, what do you say to someone who is grieving? How can your words contribute to the healing process? Or is this a situation where silence is truly golden?

In this book, *When Silence is Golden*, I will address those awkward moments, words, and phrases that though well-intentioned, can sting. I will show you how to offer gentler, more thoughtful ways to speak and support others through grief.

Introduction

The saying, "Silence is golden" means that it is sometimes better to remain quiet than to speak in situations that require sensitivity, respect, and understanding. In the context of death, grief, and loss, it implies that offering comfort and support through silence can be better than saying things that may unintentionally be hurtful or insensitive.

When facing death, grief, and loss, people may feel the need to offer words of comfort or support. However, sometimes words may not be enough, and silence can provide a better form of comfort. This silence can show respect, empathy, and solidarity. It can also allow for reflection and emotional processing, giving the grieving person a sense of being heard and acknowledged without the pressure to respond.

"Silence is golden" does not mean you should always remain silent or that words are not valuable. Instead, it suggests that silence can be more powerful than words in certain situations such as death, grief, and loss.

Silence can be a positive alternative to speaking out of turn when others are grieving the death of loved ones because it allows them to process their emotions and thoughts without the pressure to respond to well-intentioned but possibly hurtful comments.

When people are grieving, they may experience a range of emotions, including shock, denial, anger, sadness, and guilt. These emotions can be unpredictable and overwhelming, making it difficult to communicate effectively. In such situations, offering a supportive presence through silence can be more helpful than trying to provide words of comfort that may not be well received.

Silence can provide a safe space for grieving individuals to express their emotions, thoughts, and memories of the deceased at their own pace. It can also demonstrate respect for their need for space and privacy. This can help them feel heard and acknowledged without the pressure to respond.

It is important to note that silence does not mean ignoring grieving persons or avoiding them altogether. Instead, you can offer support through nonverbal cues such as a gentle touch, a hug, or simply sitting with them. Practical support, such as helping with household chores or running errands, can also be offered.

How Words and Actions Can Impact Those Grieving

Words and actions can significantly impact individuals who are grieving. Grief is a complex and personal process that can be influenced by various factors, including the support and understanding of others. Insensitive or hurtful words and actions can prolong the grieving process and cause additional emotional pain.

People who are grieving may be in a vulnerable and fragile state, and their reactions may not always be predictable or rational. It is essential to be mindful of what we say and do in the presence of someone who is grieving to avoid causing further distress.

Examples of How People's Words and Actions Can Affect Those Grieving

- Saying insensitive things: well-intentioned comments that are poorly worded or thoughtless can be hurtful. For example, saying "I know how you feel" or "It's God's plan" can dismiss the individual's emotions and beliefs.

- Ignoring or avoiding the person: avoiding those who are grieving or failing to acknowledge their loss can make them feel isolated and unsupported.

- Offering unsolicited advice: Grieving individuals may not be ready to hear advice on how to move on or cope with their loss. Unsolicited advice can come across as insensitive and unhelpful.

- Comparing losses: comparing losses or suggesting that one loss is more significant than another can be hurtful and dismissive of the individual's emotions.

- Acting impatient: grieving is a process that takes time, and those who are grieving may need to talk about their loss repeatedly. Acting impatient or dismissive of their need to grieve can be hurtful.

On the other hand, supportive words and actions can have a positive impact on those who are grieving. Simple acts of kindness and empathy: listening, offering practical support, and showing understanding, can go a long way in helping someone who is grieving feel supported and validated.

We must be mindful of what we say and do and offer empathy, understanding, and support to those who are going through the grieving process. The reality is that death is something we never get used to, no matter how many times it happens to us. And knowing exactly what to say is not an easy task. No matter how skilled a speaker you are, when it comes to hearing about the passing of someone, no speech equals the pain and feelings one faces. Even the greatest writers struggle to find the right words to comfort the griever. Knowledge and experience become irrelevant.

During the awkward moments of not knowing what to say, some may think it is best to say something, rather than saying nothing at all. At that moment, as they say, you may put your foot in your mouth. You may say something with good intentions that comes out completely wrong or out of place. If you have been in this situation, do not feel embarrassed, as you are not alone.

Trying to come up with the best way to support your grieving friend or family member can be very challenging. The best approach can vary depending on the individual and the nature of your relationship. From personal experience and being a grief survivor myself, I have realised there is no one-size-fits-all approach when it comes to navigating how to support loved ones.

While writing this book, I took it upon myself to conduct a small experiment with my very close and dearest friends. I value their feedback, and they have shown up for me on numerous occasions. They are the ones who will always have my back, no matter what. When I presented the question of what I should say to a grieving person or friend, their answers were similar, and they acknowledged that this is a challenging situation that many people face. They didn't know exactly what to say, but in their defence, they proceeded with the answer, "I just say something anyway, rather than stand or sit there in silence."

Another response was that saying something tends to break the quiet moment. It also implies that you are there, and you care about those who are grieving.

Some believe that silence implies disconnection and indifference. Consequently, people often resort to saying what they think the person wants to hear. We are all guilty of saying the best or worst thing to someone who is grieving in an attempt to provide comfort. We never mean to cause any harm. Due to our human instinct, we act empathetically, allowing our compassionate side to come alive. However, despite our well-intentioned gestures, certain statements can inadvertently miss the mark, causing more distress than comfort.

Words possess immense power, especially when shared during moments of sorrow. As we navigate the delicate terrain of supporting those who are grieving, it is crucial to explore the impact of commonly used phrases and how they are received by individuals experiencing loss. Although our words during times of grief are usually rooted in compassion, it is essential to recognise that sometimes, what we intend to convey and how it is perceived may differ significantly.

Before we delve into the intricacies of commonly used statements, I encourage you to take a moment to reflect on the importance of language in navigating grief. Let us consider how certain words might be received and the power they hold in shaping someone's experience of loss

CHAPTER 1

I Am Sorry
for Your Loss

Grief does not demand pity; it requests acknowledgment.
— **JUDE GIBBS**

I n life, there are moments when words fall short, and the comfort we try to offer can unintentionally cause resentment. This chapter explores situations where using the common saying, "I am sorry for your loss" to extend sympathy resulted in a reaction that was far from the expected gratitude.

Grief is a complicated mix of emotions, and it varies from person to person. The way we express condolences can provide comfort or, unfortunately, stir up emotions we never intended to awaken. This story teaches us a powerful lesson in empathy, reminding us that when faced with loss, we must choose our words carefully because they have the power to heal and hurt.

Join me as I delve into the complexity of human emotions, the unintended consequences of our well-meaning actions, and the journey of reconciliation after a well-intentioned mistake. Through this exploration, we come to understand that even the most sincere condolences can be met with unexpected challenges.

When people experience loss, whether it's the death of a loved one, the end of a relationship, or another personal setback, offering condolences is a way to validate their pain and show compassion. Simply saying, "I am sorry for your loss" carries a lot of weight and represents genuine empathy. However, while a well-intentioned expression of sympathy can be incredibly uplifting for the person grieving, there is also a flipside where such phrases may trigger deep and unexplored emotions within them.

"I am sorry for your loss" has been used to express condolences for many years. It has become deeply ingrained in our collective consciousness, passed down through generations and transcending language barriers. Like any other familiar saying, there is nothing inherently wrong with this phrase, as it genuinely conveys sorrow for the loss experienced by the bereaved individual. Its widespread usage has made it almost instinctive, a go-to response when we first hear of someone's passing. These words come easily and naturally when we want to express our sympathy.

If you find yourself using this phrase, there's no need to judge yourself. It's a well-known expression that has simply become a default response when we may not be prepared to offer something different or more personalised. However, it's important to acknowledge that this phrase, while genuine, can sound overused and generic. Though heartfelt, it lacks a personal touch and can feel clichéd to those who have heard it repeatedly.

A friend once told me, "If I had a penny for every time I heard this expression during my time of grief, I would be very wealthy by now." And I immediately understood what she meant.

"I am sorry for your loss" occupies a unique space when consoling someone who is grieving. Its impact, whether positive or negative, is strongly influenced by the nature of the loss itself and your relationship with the individual. Whether it's the loss of a job, a loved one, a relationship, or even a cherished pet, how the phrase resonates with the bereaved largely depends on the circumstances and their emotional connection to the situation. In some cases, people may find that this phrase falls short of capturing the depth of their emotions and the significance of their relationship with the person who has passed away.

Reflecting on my own experiences, I have often found myself browsing through the card section of my local shopping mall for various occasions: birthdays, weddings, anniversaries, and even funerals. However, it was after the passing of my mother that I began to pay particular attention to sympathy cards. As I opened a few of them, I couldn't help but notice the words printed on both the front cover and inside: "I am sorry for your loss."

It struck me that these cards seemed to lack a personal connection, depth, and the opportunity for genuine empathy. I couldn't help but shake my head in disbelief, and for a brief moment, a thought crossed my mind. Although I quickly dismissed that thought, the lingering question remained: had I been purchasing cards without truly grasping their profound and genuine meaning?

Instantly, a wave of guilt washed over me, and my heart sank in shame. I am fully aware of my involvement in perpetuating these traditional customs and cultural norms, and you may relate to these feelings as well. Admittedly, navigating the delicate terrain of consoling friends, colleagues, and acquaintances who are struggling with the loss of a loved one is undeniably challenging. However, we hold on to the belief that saying something, even if it's imperfect, is far better than saying nothing at all. It's a simple yet heartfelt gesture of love and an attempt to provide comfort, even though we acknowledge that these words often fall short of truly consoling the griever during this life-altering ordeal.

In keeping with tradition, my usual response would involve going to the store to purchase a sympathy card, which I would then give to the grieving family. My contribution usually amounted to signing my name at the bottom, as the card already had a pre-written message. Breaking away from ingrained cultural practices can be difficult, and it can be exceptionally challenging to break free from ingrained habits and customs. In doing so, we unintentionally put those who grieve in the tough position of having to respond with a polite "thank you," even as they struggle with overwhelming emotions and try to find the right words.

Experiencing a season of grief was a wake-up call for me, a trigger that made me realise I had been approaching things all wrong. I had unknowingly become a prisoner of tradition, a force that we often accept without questioning, simply going with the flow, as they say. Maybe you can relate; the thought may cross your mind, "Why change something that has worked for generations?" After all, there doesn't seem to be a reason to reinvent the wheel, so we find comfort in sticking to what's familiar, in repeating the same words and actions we've known for so long.

So, let's face this reality head-on: how can we restrain ourselves from breaking free from these ingrained habits and expressions in life?

The word "sorry" is often associated with feelings of pity and acknowledgement of wrongdoing. It usually involves apologizing for a mistake made or any hurt caused. However, when faced with situations like the death of a loved one or the loss of a job, marriage, or something deeply cherished, people almost always start conversations by saying, "I am sorry for your loss."

In these situations, it's important to recognise it's not your fault the person died. You are not responsible for the absence of my mother or sister; they are gone, and their return is impossible.

As I read through a majority of online articles, I stumbled upon an article with an intriguing title: "How to Convey Your Condolences Beyond 'I'm Sorry for Your Loss'." The author made a thought-provoking claim that simply saying "sorry for your loss" can seem insincere. Instead, offering a heartfelt message that goes beyond the usual condolences can truly bring comfort to those who are grieving and help them navigate their difficult journey.

I can confirm the truth of this statement. A few days after my mother passed away, I received a letter in the mail. I noticed that my address was handwritten on the envelope and immediately realised it wasn't one of the usual bills and letters I received.

As I carefully held the letter in my hands, I couldn't help but notice the address stamped in Wales. The only person I know living there is none other than my dear friend, Iphia, affectionately known as Tia in our close circle. Although we don't talk every day, our bond runs deep. In times of need, she's the one I turn to for advice or a comforting prayer. In modern language, we've got each other's backs—a rock-solid support system. She understands me, and I understand her; it's a mutual understanding that goes beyond just friendship.

Our journey began in 2008 when we met at university. It was during our very first conversation that we discovered something remarkable—we were living on the same street, just a stone's throw away from each other. From that moment on, we became more than friends; we became like family. We've been through tough times together, offering prayers when needed, shedding tears during difficult moments, and celebrating each other's successes. Our connection is unbreakable, and it goes far beyond our university days. In essence, we are an integral part of each other's lives, and no matter the physical distance between us, our friendship remains strong.

Receiving a letter from her didn't catch me off guard; after all, she had already expressed her condolences over the phone and through WhatsApp. What truly amazed me was the heartfelt contents of the envelope. It wasn't just another sympathy card; it was a handmade masterpiece. The front of the card featured a cherished photo of my mom and me during one of my visits to St. Lucia, a picture she must have "borrowed" from my

Facebook profile or a post. It was unique, different from the others I had received. While some were undoubtedly well-intentioned, they seemed somewhat repetitive, but hers stood out.

As I read the message, a sense of relief came over me. What a thoughtful and creative idea! Instead of using pre-printed messages, she put her creativity into the card, making something truly original. Her words, written with care, expressed her sympathy and unwavering support in a way I had not experienced before. They had depth and sincerity, almost making me feel her presence through the heartfelt sentiments written on that card. It was an incredibly touching gesture from both her and her family.

The words, though simple, touched a part of me and brought tears to my eyes, yet, at the same time, provided comfort. Below is the content of the card from my beloved friend.

Thinking of you, Jermila
I had my own notion of grief.
I thought it was the sad time that followed the death of someone
you love. And you have to push through it to get to the other side.
But I am learning there is no other side.
There is no pushing through but rather,
There is absorption.
There is adjustment.
There is acceptance.
And grief is not something you complete
But rather you endure.
Grief is not a task to finish and move on.
But an element of yourself

An alteration of your being.
A new way of seeing.
A new dimension to self
"Blessed are those who mourn for they shall be comforted"
(Matthew 5: 4)
Sending you love, Tia and family.

A loss is a deeply personal experience, and although it may seem similar on the surface, no two instances are ever truly the same. When someone dies, we often refer to it as a loss—a significant one at that. However, death encompasses more than just a loss; it brings with it a multitude of emotions that cannot be concealed or ignored. Instead, we must learn to navigate the unpredictable storm of grief that life has sent our way.

This journey involves adapting, finding our way, and coping with the turbulent emotions that persist despite our best efforts. Grief introduces us to denial and shock, emotions that we must confront and acknowledge. It is important to recognise that loss extends beyond death; it includes various aspects of our lives, such as relationships, jobs, health, and material possessions. Yet, we often find ourselves using the same expression, "Sorry for your loss," which, while well-intentioned, can never fully alleviate the pain an individual is experiencing in that very moment or in the moments that follow.

It took the sudden loss of my loved ones for me to truly understand how inadequate this phrase can make someone feel. There was a moment of uncomfortable silence that made me contemplate its true meaning. It couldn't bring my loved ones back or ease the overwhelming emotions I was wrestling with. So, I began to question the significance of saying, "I'm sorry for your loss." Was it meant to somehow make me feel better about the harrowing events unfolding in my life?

As I tried to make sense of it all, I reached a conclusion within me. I realised that the intention behind uttering those words is to offer support and comfort during an immensely troubling time.

Could those words alleviate my pain or erase the struggles I was facing? The answer was no, but they served as an acknowledgement of the pain and loss I was enduring. This is exactly what my friends told me when I asked them the same question.

Memories flooded back of the numerous times I had heard the phrase, "I am sorry for your loss," when people inquired about my mother's well-being, and I informed them of her passing. In response, I often found myself simply saying, "Thank you." It would roll off my tongue almost automatically, a response I chose perhaps because it seemed most polite and gracious."

Then, I remembered another occasion when I encountered those very same words. It was after an important job interview; that I had prepared for diligently for weeks. I devoted hours to studying possible interview questions, conducted thorough research on the company, stayed updated with the latest policies and procedures, and rehearsed my responses endlessly to ensure I wouldn't disappoint myself on the big day. However, my hopes were met with a phone call a few days later that began with, "Miss Sealys, let me first congratulate you on the interview. You performed exceedingly well, and it was a tough decision between you and another candidate. However, I regret to inform you that we are unable to offer you the job at this time. Please keep an eye out for other potential openings within the company."

When those words were delivered to me that day, it felt like a crushing blow, as if a bus had run me over and squashed every organ in my body. I had been eagerly anticipating that job opportunity and had poured my heart and soul into the interview. I'm sure many can relate to a time in their lives when they've heard the phrase, "I'm sorry."

That was the first time I wished I hadn't heard those words. My initial thought was, "You can't truly be sorry because if you were, I would have received the job."

I found myself consumed by a profound sense of self-disappointment. It appears as if I hadn't done enough to secure the job, that my efforts had fallen short, and all the late hours I had invested were in vain. I felt I had wasted precious time, only to be met with the disheartening news, "I'm sorry you weren't successful this time."

Those words echoed in my ears for an extended period, casting a shadow over my self-esteem. Often, I would reflect on that experience and convince myself I was a failure. It was a daunting realisation as I had a deep-seated dislike for interviews. Nevertheless, I knew they were a necessary step on the path to employment.

You might be wondering, what do you say when "sorry for your loss" feels inadequate? Truthfully, there may never be perfect words to offer during such times. Overthinking and striving for the perfect words can be counterproductive. However, as promised, by the end of this chapter, I will share ways in which you can express your empathy and support to a grieving friend or family member.

It's undoubtedly challenging to stand by in silence. As humans, we've been taught and believe that it's necessary to say something when someone in our circle is in pain and grieving. Many agree that offering words of comfort serves as a genuine demonstration of care for our loved ones. Additionally, it's seen as a sign of respect and consideration for the grieving person's feelings and emotions.

It's important to remember that the person who is grieving may experience a wide range of emotions and reactions. Grief is a deeply personal and individual journey, so how a griever responds when hearing these words can vary significantly. While some may find great comfort in such expressions, others may have more complex reactions. Sensitivity to the individual's needs and emotions is crucial. Give those who are grieving a safe space to express themselves in their own way, whether that involves discussing their grief or simply accepting condolences with a nod or a thank you.

There are many reasons why people who are grieving may struggle with accepting condolences. For some, it is due to the intense and overwhelming emotions they experience during their grief, such as sadness, anger, guilt, or numbness. When someone offers condolences, it can trigger these emotions and bring them to the surface, making it challenging for the griever to respond. During the early stages of grief, individuals are still in a state of shock and disbelief. They may not fully comprehend the reality of their loss, and hearing condolences can serve as a painful reminder of what has happened. They may feel over-whelmed by constant encounters with well-wishers and condolences, which can be exhausting.

Responding to individual expressions of sympathy can also be emotionally draining. The bereaved might find it difficult to express their emotions openly, especially during a time of profound sadness. They may struggle to find the right words to respond adequately to condolences. There is also the fear of breaking down in front of others, which may lead to judgement and being considered weak. Those who grieve may prefer to do so privately and may not want to discuss their feelings with others, even well-meaning friends, and family. They may interpret condolences as an intrusion into their private space.

In the journey of grief, it's important to recognise that not everyone may readily accept help or support. Some grievers may strongly believe in handling their grief independently, fearing that they could burden those around them with their pain. It's a complex situation where the dynamics of grief often take unexpected turns.

At times, grief manifests as anger. Those who are grieving may find themselves consumed by anger directed at the world or harbouring resentment toward expressions of sympathy. To them, condolences might seem like empty gestures that fail to address the depth of their pain.

Grief not only takes an emotional toll but can also have physical effects. It can leave grievers feeling utterly drained, lacking the energy required for engaging in conversations or even responding to condolences. The exhaustion can be overwhelming, leaving little room for interaction.

Cultural and personal beliefs and norms play a significant role in shaping how grievers respond to condolences. Different cultures have specific customs and rituals surrounding grief, and individuals may have unique preferences for how they wish to be comforted. It's a reminder that understanding and respecting these differences is paramount when offering support during the grieving journey.

It is important to approach those who are grieving with sensitivity and respect for their individual needs and preferences. While offering condolences is a way of demonstrating support and care, it's equally important to allow grievers the necessary time and space to process their grief in their own manner. Simply being available for support, even without words, can sometimes be the most significant gesture during a person's grieving process. Here are some specific ways to support someone who is grieving:

- Be Present: sometimes, the most powerful form of condolence is simply being present for the bereaved. Offering a compassionate presence, lending an empathetic ear, and providing a safe space for them to share their emotions can be immensely comforting during their time of loss.

- Empathy and Active Listening: the foundation of offering condolences lies in empathising with the bereaved's emotions. Listening actively and without judgement allows them to share their feelings and memories, fostering a sense of support and understanding.

- Thoughtful Words: choosing the right words can make a significant difference. Expressions such as "I am deeply sorry for your loss" or "My condolences to you and your family" convey sincere sympathy and a sense of shared grief.

- Honouring the Deceased: remembering those who passed away by sharing anecdotes or highlighting their positive qualities can bring comfort to the grieving individual. Offering specific memories or stories shows that their loved one's life was valued and appreciated.

- Practical Support: in addition to verbal expressions, offering practical assistance can alleviate some of the burdens faced by those grieving. Actions such as preparing meals, running errands, or providing a listening ear can demonstrate genuine care and help ease the grieving process.

- Cultural Sensitivity in Condolences: different cultures and traditions have varying approaches to expressing condolences. Be aware of and respect these cultural nuances when offering sympathy. Taking the time to learn about specific customs or traditions can show respect and sensitivity toward the grieving person's cultural background.

Expressions of condolence play a significant role in offering sympathy for someone's loss. They serve as a crucial support system for those going through the difficult journey of grief. By understanding the importance of empathy, choosing thoughtful words, and being present for the bereaved, we can make a profound impact. This can provide solace and remind them that they are not alone in their sorrow.

While saying, "I am sorry for your loss" is well-intentioned, it is often inadequate. Throughout this chapter, I have uncovered the range of emotions that accompany grief and loss, acknowledging that there is no one-size-fits-all approach to consoling someone in their time of need.

Although "I am sorry for your loss" is a traditional and commonly used expression of sympathy, we now understand that it may not fully satisfy everyone. Grief is a deeply personal journey, and each person's experience of it can vary greatly. While these words may genuinely comfort some individuals, others may have more complex reactions.

It's essential to remember that there are no perfect words that can magically ease the pain of grief. What matters most is the intention behind our words and our ability to create a safe space for the grieving person to express their emotions and thoughts in their own way.

Toolkit of Meaningful Gestures

While "I am sorry for your loss" is a commonly used expression of sympathy, there are many other ways to convey your condolences and support to someone who is grieving. By using different words and phrases, you can offer comfort in a more personalised and heartfelt manner. Here are some alternative ways to express your sympathy:

- **My deepest condolences**: this phrase emphasises the depth of your sympathy.

- **You have my heartfelt sympathies**: this conveys that your condolences come from the heart.

- **I'm here for you**: this expresses your willingness to provide support and assistance to the grieving person.

- **I can't imagine what you're going through, but I'm here to help**: this acknowledges the difficulty of the situation and your commitment to being there for the bereaved.

- **Sending you love and strength during this difficult time:** this emphasises emotional support and resilience.

- **May you find peace and comfort**: this expresses a wish for the grieving person's well-being.

- **My thoughts are with you**: this phrase conveys that you are thinking about the bereaved and their loss.

- **Wishing you strength and healing in the days ahead**: these express hope for the person's emotional healing.

- **You and your family are in my prayers**: this shows spiritual or religious support.

- **I'm here to listen if you want to talk**: this offers a listening ear and a safe space for the bereaved to share their feelings.

- **Please accept my sympathies**: a more formal way to express condolences.

- **You have my deepest sympathy**: another way to emphasise the depth of your condolences.

- **I share in your sorrow**: this expresses your connection to their grief.

- **I'm thinking of you and your family**: this shows concern for the well-being of the entire family.

- **May the memories of your loved one bring you comfort**: this focuses on the positive memories and the role they can play in healing.

- **I wish I had the right words to say**: acknowledging the difficulty of finding words to console.

- **Your loved one will be greatly missed**: this acknowledges the significance of the person who has passed away.

- **I'm here to help with anything you need**: offering practical support and assistance.

Remember that the most important thing is to offer your condolences sincerely and with empathy. The specific words you choose should reflect your genuine care and support for those who are grieving.

POWERFUL CHAPTER TAKEAWAYS

1. Understanding that grief varies from person to person is essential. Some may find great comfort in hearing those words, while others may have complex reactions. What truly matters is the intention behind our words and actions, as well as our ability to provide a safe space for grieving individuals to express their emotions in their own way.

2. Our toolkit of meaningful gestures and alternative words offers a range of ways to provide comfort and support during the challenging journey of grief. By actively listening, offering specific help, sharing memories, and using empathetic words, among other gestures, we can demonstrate our care and compassion effectively.

3. Ultimately, the takeaway is that when "I am sorry for your loss" falls short, we can offer more meaningful and personalised support. By doing so, we can be a source of genuine solace and companionship for those navigating the difficult path of grief.

CHAPTER 2

I Know Exactly How You Feel

While we may walk similar paths, each journey through grief is as unique as a fingerprint. What I can offer is a hand to hold along the way.
— UNKNOWN.

I n this chapter, we are exploring the common phrase, "I know exactly how you feel." This expression is often used to convey condolences, empathy, and the idea that someone understands what we are going through, especially when dealing with grief. But given that grief is a personal experience, can we truly understand the other person's feelings?

While we may share the general grief of losing the same person, our grief may manifest differently. We might grieve at varying depths because nobody else can measure how much we love or admire the person we lost. Even if multiple people loved the same individual, the nature and depth of that love can vary significantly because not everyone expresses their love or grief in the same way.

Consider the scenario where two people have a mutual friend, but one of them has a much deeper bond with that friend. In such cases, it is challenging to truly empathise with the depth of the other person's grief. Often, we grieve silently, holding onto our love for the departed person, knowing that no one else can fully comprehend it. Sometimes, we may refrain from expressing condolences to the family, even though we loved the person deeply because it may not be perceived as our place to do so.

Saying, "I know exactly how you feel," can unintentionally downplay people's grief because, in reality, we cannot fully grasp the depth of their emotions. While we may have a sense of their pain because we are grieving too, the profoundness of love we hold for someone dictates how we grieve, whether silently or openly, covertly, or overtly.

It was only after losing my mother and sister that I truly understood the unique and indescribable nature of the emotions that come with grief and loss. I realised that the waves of emotion I was feeling were deeply personal and impossible to fully convey or share with others. The moment I felt I couldn't go on without my mother was a battle that consumed me day and night. Even though my siblings were grieving at the same time, we couldn't share or feel each other's pain.

Our relationships with our departed loved ones were distinct and personal. Each of us loved them in our own unique ways and mourned and grieved for them individually. We couldn't compare or measure the depth of our love or the extent of our pain. What we missed about them and the memories we held were entirely different from one another. As a result, our grief was a totally isolated experience, unique to each of us.

I struggle with anger, denial, shock, guilt, and various other emotions. How could anyone understand unless they were the ones facing these uncertain emotions and pain? Only through my firsthand experience with grief and loss did I gain a new-found appreciation for the profound emotions and thoughts that accompany such a significant loss. I regretted my lack of consideration toward others who were grieving in the past.

I wanted to appear supportive, but the truth is I didn't know what they were going through because I hadn't been in that situation. I hadn't gone through the process and had no personal understanding of that pain. However, now that I have experienced the pain of losing loved ones, I can provide insight into why certain statements are not supportive when someone you know is grieving the loss of a loved one. To my friends, family, loved ones, and even to you, the reader, I deeply apologise for the damage or hurt we may have caused with such statements.

All too often, those who are grieving have heard the words, "I know exactly how you are feeling" or "I know how you feel." I had a rude awakening when people said those words to me. The truth is that nobody truly understands the depth of what you are experiencing during those painful times in your life.

I experienced a mixture of surprise and anger because the loss wasn't theirs. It wasn't their loved one, and their feelings couldn't match mine in the same way, so how could they know how I felt? However, in my anger, I soon realised I wasn't any different. When my friends or acquaintances went through their own grieving experiences, I used those exact words. As I reviewed messages I had sent over the years, I noticed this recurring pattern. It felt like a simple copy-and-paste response, lacking the authenticity I had hoped to convey.

I said those words simply because I grew up hearing them. They rolled off my tongue as easily as reciting nursery rhymes or multiplication tables. I didn't know any better, and I never really thought about their impact. But now, having experienced grief and loss firsthand, I find myself questioning whether I ever truly understood how others felt when they lost loved ones. Did I genuinely grasp their pain, even though I had been through loss and grief many times myself?

Each time a loved one dies; the pain feels different and more intense. Each loss carries its unique set of emotions and experiences. It has become clear to me that, while I may have empathised before, I couldn't fully comprehend the depth of their sorrow until I walked the same path myself.

Tradition and culture can indeed play a significant role in how we approach and support the bereaved. However, they can sometimes hinder our ability to provide effective support. There are several reasons for this. For instance, the fear of "reinventing the wheel" or abandoning long-held traditions can be a barrier to adopting more modern and effective approaches to support-ing those who grieve. Updating cultural practices and beliefs takes time and effort.

Another reason is struggling to find the right words. People may resort to familiar phrases and clichés because they lack the vocabulary or emotional intelligence to navigate conversations related to death more effectively.

Additionally, as human beings, we are creatures of habit. We often find it difficult to accept changes, especially when it comes to deeply ingrained cultural practices. We may be reluctant to deviate from traditional ways of coping with grief because they provide a sense of stability and predictability in times of emotional turmoil.

As knowledge and understanding of grief continue to develop, societies must adapt and embrace new approaches that prioritise the needs and well-being of the bereaved. The emphasis should be placed on encouraging open and empathetic communication, providing resources and education on grief support, and being willing to modify traditions when they no longer serve their intended purpose or exclude certain individuals. The goal should be to create an environment where grievers feel genuinely cared for and supported during their difficult times.

Understanding the depth of someone's experience during their grieving process is a challenge that we may never fully conquer. It's crucial to always keep in mind that the person who knows their grief best is the one going through it—the bereaved themselves. I may have touched upon this concept in my previous book, emphasising that each person's grief is as unique as a fingerprint, possessing an entirely personal DNA.

In my journey, I found myself utterly perplexed by the wild sea of emotions that engulfed me. The struggle was real—the heartache, pain, burden of guilt and denial, and the ever-shifting waves of emotions. It was a complex and deeply personal experience that defied any attempt to neatly fit it into a one-size-fits-all framework.

How can we possibly diminish people's feelings by presuming to understand precisely how they feel, especially when we have no insight into the depth of emotions they are struggling with? It's an impossible task. Regardless of how many times one experiences the loss of a loved one, coming to terms with grief, loss, and death is tough. In every instance, every individual is profoundly different.

The revisitation of these emotions can have an enduring impact, causing emotional paralysis and shattered spirits. Through my own journey with grief, I have learned valuable lessons along the way. One of the most significant is the importance of avoiding passing judgement. We should never assume that we fully understand someone's experience just because we have been through a similar situation. It is necessary not to downplay someone else's grief or make it about ourselves. We are not equipped to truly understand their genuine emotions, so we should approach their pain with empathy, humility, and open hearts.

As I continue my journey with grief, I realise that I haven't fully grasped all there is to know about it. On that particular day, as I stood there, seemingly frozen in my tracks, I had a realisation. In the past, I unintentionally deprived someone of their genuine feelings and emotions by trying to relate their experiences to my own. It was an eye-opening moment that filled me with a sense of shame. I understood that what I had learned from society many years ago may not be the right way to approach such delicate matters.

This revelation made me question the traditions and teachings that have been passed down through generations. It made me realise that not everything handed down the line is inherently right or wrong. So, how do we bring about change? How do we embark on the journey of better educating the generation that follows us and challenging the perspectives of those who came before us?

The answer lies in acknowledging that the study and research of grief and loss should be an ongoing, evolving endeavour, just like other areas of life. We need to reframe and rethink how we communicate with those who are grieving. By constantly seeking new insights, sharing experiences, and engaging in open conversations about grief, we can challenge outdated norms and provide better support to those in need. It's a process of growth and learning that can lead to more empathetic and compassionate ways of connecting with one another during times of sorrow.

Many of us are familiar with the sayings, "Mother knows best" and "It is so because I said it is." Society has taught us the importance of respecting our elders, believing that the older generation imparts wisdom from their wealth of knowledge and experience. However, I question the idea that age automatically equates to experience.

What truly qualifies as valuable experience is not just the passing of time, but the actual lived experiences and the realisation that we may have been wrong in our approaches to certain situations.

I have come to understand the discomfort that grievers often feel. Instead of confronting us and telling us we're wrong, they tend to choose silence, not wanting to offend us with their true thoughts. They may find themselves at a loss for words, struggling with the chaos that grief has brought into their lives.

It's important to recognise that their lack of acknowledgment or a simple response like "It's fine" is not meant to be rude.

In those awkward moments, they are engaged in an internal struggle, trying to make sense of their own whirlwind of emotions. They are essentially on a battlefield, playing a game of hide and seek with their formidable opponent— grief. While I can relate to their struggle, I cannot claim to fully understand their exact emotions. Grief, after all, is an unrelenting tug of war between the pain that tightens its grip on our hearts and the battle to stay strong and avoid appearing vulnerable.

No one can ever truly fathom the exact depths of another person's feelings. I vividly remember a moment when I fought the urge to shout at the top of my lungs, "No, you don't!" Instead, I chose to walk away in silence. While it might have seemed, I was ungrateful for the support someone was offering, my decision to remain silent was driven by the need to avoid saying something hurtful or inappropriate.

At that particular moment, I realised that I may have unintentionally hurt many friends and family members with this seemingly innocent phrase. It made me reflect on how easily we might have used such words ourselves, not fully grasping the impact they could have on others. Another common occurrence is when someone starts sharing their own experience while someone else is grieving. While this may be done with good intentions, possibly to demonstrate understanding or build common ground, extreme caution should be exercised. The focus immediately shifts from the bereaved to you, making them feel the attention is no longer on their pain and the profound experience they are going through. It eventually makes it about your own pain and, in the process, dims the significance of what they are enduring during this life-altering situation.

Saying that you understand how they feel can unintentionally fuse their distress. In such moments, what they truly need is someone who will simply be there for them and genuinely listen. During these times, people long for a compassionate presence that allows them to freely express their emotions as they struggle with the pain they're holding inside.

Alternatively, they might prefer to sit together in silence as they come to terms with the reality that someone they deeply cared about has passed away. During this critical time, it becomes paramount for them to sense your unwavering care and concern, to feel that you are fully present for them and that their experiences and emotions matter. Do not shift the focus to yourself and your experiences. The essence of support lies in making the bereaved feel comfortable and reassured that you are there to stand with them through their journey, acknowledging that whatever they are going through holds immense significance.

In 2020, days after the passing of my mother, I received a voice note from someone who shared their own experience of a similar loss. They claimed to know exactly how I felt and what I was going through. They proceeded to offer advice on how they had coped with their own loss, recommending actions like reading a particular book and engaging in a 40-day prayer and fasting.

I felt a surge of anger, frustration, and sadness. My grief was still raw, and I was struggling to come to terms with the fact that I had just lost my mother. She was my best friend, my heart, and my queen. She meant so much to me. And the idea of praying for 40 days felt like an inadequate response to the profound loss I had experienced. My mind was cloudy, and praying was the last thing I thought about when I had more pressing matters to attend to. For instance, arranging the funeral and worrying about whether I would be able to travel or not as it was during the COVID-19 pandemic.

The focus shifted away from me and my bereavement, and I was compelled to listen to a voice recording. The person was trying to draw parallels between their past grief, which it seemed they hadn't completely healed from, and my current experience. This approach wasn't helpful at all.

During times of grief, people don't necessarily seek solutions or advice; what they truly long for are those who will listen. They become immediate listeners themselves, putting aside their own feelings and emotions. It's in these moments that a comforting presence, a listening ear, and a gentle hug are invaluable. They need the reassurance that you genuinely care and are there to support them. Lectures and attempts to fix things aren't what grieving individuals need; they need to feel loved and heard.

It's evident that even when two people share a similar story such as both losing their mothers, sisters, fathers, or other family members, the complexity of the human mind or brain means that the difference in our individual feelings and emotions remains distinct. We can never truly grasp the full range of emotions people are simultaneously navigating. Merely being able to share a similar experience doesn't give us the ability to fully comprehend what they are truly going through.

Emotions are undeniably complex, and psychologists have identified six fundamental emotions as the foundation for the broader spectrum of our emotional experiences. These core emotions include happiness, anger, fear, sadness, surprise, and disgust. It is suggested that all other emotions we encounter stem from these six primary emotional states. Different regions of the brain are associated with processing these core emotions.

This complexity is especially evident when we consider the emotional responses triggered by grief. Grief is a multifaceted and intricate emotional experience that can manifest in various ways and hit us at different stages, sometimes all at once. The intricate web of emotions that emerge during grief undermines its profound and deeply personal nature.

I'm sure that anyone who has experienced grief can relate to the uncertainty of their own feelings, let alone understanding what others are going through. We must acknowledge that most of the time, our friends, family, and those supporting us mean well with their words and actions, even though they may unintentionally cause harm, which by no means was intentional.

Friends often want to offer comfort and support, but they frequently struggle with not knowing how to best provide that help. During these moments, we find ourselves at a loss for words, and rather than saying nothing, we end up saying something—often inadvertently causing more distress. It's a situation where, as the saying goes, we end up "shooting ourselves in the foot."

For those who have navigated this territory successfully, that's great. However, we must learn from our mistakes and accept that most of the time, we are indeed at a loss for words. Our vocabulary may fail us, and we may struggle to find the right things to say. But through awareness and empathy, we can better support those who are grieving without unintentionally causing further pain.

While grief is a universal human experience, it remains intensely personal and individualised. Let us move away from classic phrases, "I know how you feel" or "I feel your pain," as they may undermine the uniqueness of each person's grief journey. Instead, we should offer our support and presence, allowing them to express their emotions and honouring the deeply personal nature of their grief.

This reminds me of a significant moment during my nursing training when we covered the topic of pain assessment. I vividly recall the definition our lecturer shared with us that day: "Pain is what the patient says it is and exists whenever the patient says it does" (McCaffery, 1968). This definition underscores the subjective and deeply personal nature of pain, emphasising the paramount importance of believing the patients. After all, they are the sole individuals who can properly describe their own experiences.

I draw upon this perspective to argue that the feelings and emotions we go through during grief are similarly unique and intensely personal. Just as with pain, no one else can fully understand or define our grief experience. It is something only we can do.

During my time as a nursing student, there was a memorable incident that comes to mind. A patient repeatedly requested pain relief, emphasising the excruciating pain he was enduring. We had already administered the maximum allowable dosage of pain relief medication within 24 hours, and he had also taken every available pain medication in addition to his regular ones. However, his pain persisted.

During the shift handover, the nurses expressed scepticism, suggesting that the patient might be exaggerating his pain. They found it hard to believe that he was genuinely experiencing such severe discomfort, especially when another patient in the same room, who had undergone the same procedure, wasn't requesting as much pain relief. Assumptions were made, and doubts were cast on the authenticity of his pain, although we couldn't truly comprehend his feelings or what he was going through.

We immediately assumed that he was developing an addiction to the medication. However, the reality was that his pain threshold was distinct from the other patient's, and what he was feeling was deeply personal and subjective. Only he could accurately convey the sensations coursing through his body and how much pain he could endure. Regrettably, we judged him without truly knowing the intensity of his experience.

This parallels situations where people are grieving, particularly when we are aware of someone else with a similar narrative. It can be difficult to fathom why one person takes longer to reach a point of acceptance in the grief journey than another.

No one can accurately pinpoint or fully describe another person's pain or emotions when dealing with loss. Sometimes, not even the bereaved can articulate what they are experiencing. The emotional landscape is uniquely personal, and even within the same household, grieving the same loss, individuals may have entirely different emotional responses.

I experienced this phenomenon during the passing of my loved ones. The pain I felt varied from one loss to another, influenced significantly by my distinct relationships with each individual.

The intensity of the pain I struggled with and the emotions I confronted during the sudden deaths of my mom and sister felt far more profound compared to what I experienced for my aunt, uncle, cousin, and grandmother. Yet, it seemed that everyone around me kept expressing they knew exactly how I felt, often suggesting that I should forget my loss and move forward.

The truth is you cannot move forward until you allow yourself to experience and process what your body and emotions demand. There were moments when I fervently wished I could somehow transfer those feelings to others whenever they claimed to understand my experience. I longed for an exchange to occur, believing that only then would they truly comprehend the depth of what I was going through.

Within my family, we each expressed our pain and sorrow differently. Some cried openly, while others did not shed tears, but it did not mean they were not suffering. Our coping mechanisms were personal. Despite experiencing the same loss on the same day, our individual feelings and experiences were unique.

We understood that it was impossible to compare our feelings because we could not fully grasp what each family member was experiencing during that difficult period. While it may seem as if someone is putting on a display with emotional outbursts and behaviours, we must recognise that these are often unique expressions. Let me share a personal experience: when my mother passed away, there was a particular aunt of ours who would frequently break into tears, followed by loud and passionate screaming. I did not entirely grasp the depth of her emotions because I did not fully understand the bond between her and my mother. However, I came to realise that her outpouring of pain was her own way of coping. She alone knew the extent of her loss and the value of their connection. I could not deny her the authenticity of her emotions, nor could I claim to fully comprehend how she felt. Over time, I have learned that at every funeral, there is usually one distinct voice that stands out with passionate expressions of grief, and I now understand that this was her way of mourning and expressing her pain.

No matter how much you think the grief your friend or loved one is experiencing is similar to someone else's, do not make comparisons. You may have gone through grief yourself and have certain expectations about how the griever should feel. However, it is not your responsibility to "fix" the person's grief because there is no cure or quick fix for these complex emotions.

Grief has no set timeframe or schedule, and there's no definitive endpoint or final stage. Grievers may cry or not, feel anger, sadness, and a myriad of mixed emotions. None of these responses are wrong or unusual. They are all natural reactions to grief as individuals adjust to the life-altering event that has just occurred. Offer your support and understanding without imposing any expectations or comparisons.

In many instances, simply being there for your friends, family, relatives, or coworkers can be incredibly impactful. Your physical presence often speaks louder than words. Being there to offer a comforting hug can convey a sense of reassurance and let them know you truly care about their struggles. Allow them the space to express themselves without interruption or judgement, encouraging them to share their feelings. When they trust you enough to confide in you, make sure you're present and ready to listen attentively.

During times of grief and loss, all we really yearn for is an open ear, someone who will genuinely listen without the urge to interject or share their own experiences.

I can vividly recall being asked, "How are you holding up?" or "How are you feeling today?" and "How is your family coping?" These questions are thoughtful and serve as conversation starters, no doubt. However, what often troubles me is when the inquiries come in the form of text or WhatsApp messages. When you respond, there's often a noticeable pause from the sender's end. Sometimes, it takes hours or even days before you receive another reply, which can feel isolating.

I understand that life can get busy, but if you don't have a few moments to truly listen, it's better not to initiate communication in the first place. This is why there have been instances when I replied, "I'm okay," even though deep down, I really wanted to open up to someone and say, "I'm not feeling great right now." There were moments when I needed someone to lend an ear without immediately shifting the focus to their own needs. I yearned to share my feelings and offload the emotions that sometimes became too overwhelming for me. I was navigating through unfamiliar territories with my emotions as I was trying to make sense of them.

At times, you may encounter someone at the supermarket, church, bus stop, shopping mall, or even at work, and a conversation about your recent loss might be initiated in a bustling environment. The person might say, "I heard the sad news." Honestly, such places are not conducive to having deep and meaningful conversations. Firstly, these environments are typically busy, filled with unfamiliar faces and distractions. Secondly, you may have only stepped out quickly to the supermarket with limited time on your hands. Thirdly, discussing personal emotions at work is generally inappropriate, especially when there are professional responsibilities to uphold and policies in place.

It's essential to maintain professionalism, particularly in front of clients or during work-related interactions.

Changing this kind of attitude can be difficult, especially since we often haven't been taught how to address and provide support in such situations. It's something we wish we had learned at home, in school, at church, or even in our workplaces. I understand that discussing grief and loss is incredibly challenging, and it can be even more daunting to find the right place to have these conversations.

There's a common belief that sharing a personal story can help someone else going through a similar situation. However, there are times when sharing such stories can inadvertently make others feel invalidated as if their emotions and feelings don't matter. It might come across as if what they're experiencing isn't unique or special. What's important to remember is that this is a new and often bewildering experience for the person going through it. They're trying to adapt and make sense of their circumstances, constantly seeking answers.

As we strive to normalise conversations about grief, it's essential to change the way we offer support to those experiencing it. There are various meaningful ways to communicate our presence and care. Instead of assuming we fully understand someone's grief, we can express empathy by saying, "I can only imagine what you're going through, but please know I'm here for you if you need me." However, please ensure that you are really going to be there if the person needs you. Furthermore, you can send personalised messages to let the bereaved know you are thinking of them. This can be profoundly comforting. These messages demonstrate that we've taken the time to reach out specifically to them.

Let your silence be golden by listening. Beyond mere words, it's vital to actively listen when they wish to talk. Encourage them to share their feelings and experiences, assuring them that you're there to listen and support them throughout their grieving process.

Toolkit of Meaningful Gestures

Certainly, expressing empathy and understanding without directly saying "I feel your pain" can be more thoughtful and considerate. Here are some alternative ways to convey your empathy:

- "I can't imagine what you're going through, but I'm here for you."
- "I understand that this must be incredibly difficult for you."
- "My heart goes out to you during this challenging time."
- "I'm here to support you in any way you need."
- "I want you to know that I care about your well-being."
- "I'm here to listen if you ever want to talk."
- "I can't fully understand your feelings, but I'm here to help."
- "Your pain is your own, but I'm here to share the burden."
- "I can't pretend to know exactly how you feel, but I'm here to support you."
- "Your emotions are valid, and I'm here to stand by you."

These alternatives demonstrate your compassion and willingness to be there for the bereaved without assuming their feelings or minimising their unique experience of grief or hardship.

POWERFUL CHAPTER TAKEAWAYS

1. The emotions and feelings of the person going through grief are highly subjective and deeply personal at that moment.

2. The bereaved require listening ears, not advice or personal anecdotes. Provide them with the time and space to truly open up about their exact feelings.

3. Let them feel this moment is entirely about them, where they are genuinely being heard. No matter what you say, the bereaved will experience pain, a range of emotions, and heartache. Your mere presence can be a source of immense strength for them.

4. Remember, not knowing what to say in such moments doesn't make you a bad friend. Admit you do not have all the answers, but you can genuinely empathise with what they're going through. Reassure them that it's perfectly okay to feel the way they do; their emotions are entirely normal.

CHAPTER 3

They Are in a Better Place

You cannot truly heal from a loss
until you allow yourself to really feel the loss
— **MANDY HALE**

I f it takes death for someone to be in a better place, then every one of us should die and go to that better place. Is it that you get to the "good place" only by dying? Is that the only way you get to experience a better place? Why are we still here enduring the harshness of life if there is somewhere much better to be? Isn't it unfair for me, for us to be left here to experience the pain of life if death takes us to a better place?

The phrase "in a better place" is often used in the context of grief to suggest that the deceased person is in a more peaceful or happier state after death. It's an effort to offer comfort to those who are grieving by implying that the person who passed away is no longer suffering or facing the challenges of life on Earth.

Be sensitive when using this phrase because it can have different meanings and interpretations, depending on people's beliefs and cultural backgrounds. Some people find it comforting, while others may not share the same belief or may find it dismissive of their grief. So, consider the person's feelings and beliefs when using such expressions during moments of grief.

When we lose our loved ones, we often find it immensely challenging to come to terms with the pain and grief we're left with. I'm quite certain that many would prefer to be in that better place, free from the anguish and suffering that death leaves in its wake. The awkwardness, disbelief, pain, and turmoil of life can be overwhelming. Given the choice, most of us would probably trade the uncertainty of life, with its sickness, wars, anger, and pandemics, for the supposed serenity of that "better place." Wouldn't you agree?

I would indeed choose that better place over experiencing the torment of grief. Grief is the overwhelming emotion we struggle with when we lose a loved one, and it's a journey no one really prepares us for. It's a challenge that tests our humanity and is perhaps the most formidable battle one can ever face.

Grief, though invisible, is undeniably real. It cannot be hidden from or escaped; it unfailingly finds us and becomes a constant companion. Given this reality, many, like me, might echo the sentiment that they'd rather be in that better place than remain here to confront the daily struggles and the uncertain nature of grief.

Interestingly, even those who do not believe in an afterlife often hold a concept of a better place, revealing a common thread between believers and non-believers alike.

When we receive the news of the passing of someone who was battling a long illness, it's common for us to think the person is now in a better place. Some may also say, "Thank God they no longer suffer" or "God knows best." While these sentiments may hold truth for the deceased person, those who are left behind to carry on with the void and the painful emotions stemming from the loss often find it incredibly challenging to move forward.

In accordance with biblical beliefs, it's understood that a person's lifeless body rests in a state of sleep until the day of judgement. Among fellow believers, there's often the comforting notion that you will be reunited with the departed person upon the second coming of Jesus. However, this sentiment is frequently followed by a conditional "but" or "if."

The condition is that the departed person must have accepted Christ before death and had the opportunity to repent and receive salvation from God.

On December 24, 2022, during our fellowship lunch at my church, a group of us engaged in a discussion about the challenges people face when trying to support someone who is silently grieving. This conversation began when a few ladies decided to leave after their meal to visit someone who had recently experienced a loss. During the discussion, I expressed my view that while it's truly heart-warming to have individuals visit you during your time of grief, there's one aspect I find less favourable: when members of the church family come over and open the Bible.

Based on my own experiences, I deeply appreciated the presence of people in our home when I lost my family members. However, I felt quite uncomfortable when they asked me about my favourite song. At that exact moment, my mind and thoughts were racing as I tried to come to terms with my loss. The singing and Bible reading almost made me feel like I was inside a church, attending a full church service.

I understand that people mean well and want to offer spiritual support to those grieving, but immediately after the death of a loved one may not be the right time to have a complete church service.

This situation can intensify the anger someone may already be feeling toward God. Personally, I was already struggling with questions about God's fairness and justice, questioning why such tragedy had befallen me. I asked God questions that seemed to go unanswered, unable to hear His voice or sense His presence.

My church family's comforting words and texts couldn't penetrate the fog in my mind, nor could they reach and console me. My anger toward God intensified because I had asked for prayers, particularly for my mother, and it seemed as though He had not answered them or those of my church family. Yet, He directed them to come to my home, singing and telling me that He cares and will take care of me. Although I knew these words to be true, in my current state of mind, I couldn't process them as such.

One of my friends shared a heartbreaking memory from the time when her mother passed away. She recounted how, during the visits of well-wishers, one lady asked her, "Was your mother saved?" Essentially, the question was meant to inquire if her mother was a born-again Christian or a follower of Jesus. My friend explained how she felt this question was deeply inappropriate at the time. Even though years have passed since then, what struck her most was the hurt caused by someone thinking it was acceptable to ask such a question at that time.

The deep hurt this incident left with her stemmed from the suggestion that her mother did not meet the criteria for life after death, perhaps implying her soul was forever lost. As Christians, we must be mindful of our comments, especially when our religious views differ from those of the deceased. After all, who are we to claim we fully understand someone's relationship with the Lord?

Our primary responsibility in such situations should be to offer support and post-loss care for the grieving person, should they need it, rather than passing judgement on their loved one's spiritual beliefs or status.

A couple of days ago, I was caring for a patient who had been admitted due to suicidal thoughts and self-harm. During our conversation, I gradually became aware that she had recently lost a friend and, troublingly, believed herself to be responsible for her friend's death. This belief had pushed her to the point of not wanting to live any longer.

While my professional instincts urged me to inquire why she thought she was the cause of her friend's passing and to gather as much information as possible for assessment, I consciously made a different choice. Instead, I decided to let her speak, knowing that in this critical moment, allowing her to express her feelings and thoughts was more important than strictly adhering to a clinical assessment.

Given my personal experiences with grief, I chose to simply be the listening ear that was desperately needed. Grief, as I understand it, is not a medical condition that can be easily fixed. It remains a rather taboo subject, and even though research has made progress, the fundamental emotional needs of individuals in grief often go unaddressed.

As healthcare professionals, we sometimes miss the signs of grief because it's such a complex and multifaceted experience. There's a tendency to focus on treating the physical symptoms, inadvertently neglecting the profound emotional aspect of grief.

In the case I mentioned earlier, due to her suicidal ideation, she was referred to a mental health specialist as she was considered a threat to herself and potentially to others. However, it became apparent that her cry for help ran much deeper than what was initially visible. She was burdened with a sense of guilt for something entirely beyond her control.

Driven by the well-intentioned but misguided reassurances from her friends and family about her deceased friend being in a "better place now," she had developed a belief that if she attempted suicide, she would join her friend in that supposedly better place. In her mind, this was her way of confirming that her friend was indeed okay, and she, too, would be okay because she'd be reunited with her best friend.

Her relationship with her friend was incredibly close and practically perfect. As best friends, they shared everything in life—from shopping to school and holidays, they did it all together. The thought of living life without the person who had been her constant companion in all these activities was unimaginable. The weight of living while her friend had passed away felt unbearable, leaving her with no compelling reason to continue.

As I was working on this book, I conducted several Google searches on the most hurtful things people have been told while grieving, and the phrase "He/she is in a better place" kept appearing. This reinforced the idea that I wasn't alone in feeling hurt by a comment that was intended to provide comfort. In one of the articles I came across, the author emphasised the importance of being cautious with such statements, as they can have a profound impact on the grieving individual. In some cases, the person grieving might even contemplate ending their own life in the hope of being reunited with their loved ones in that supposed better place.

The comment can often come across as unintentionally insulting as if implying that the life the person was living was a nightmarish existence. It may inadvertently suggest that the time spent alive, regardless of the circumstances or lifestyle, wasn't worth much. However, the reality is that no matter the condition or lifestyle of those who died, the pain of their loss remains profoundly felt by their loved ones.

My concern with this idea is that I would much prefer to have my mother and sister right here beside me. If, indeed, they are in a better place, then it might lead one to question why we shouldn't all pass away and join them, considering this place is supposed to be a paradise. When I think of a "better place," I can't help but imagine a location in line with our most cherished dreams—the perfect holiday destination, where relaxation involves soaking up the sun and lounging on a beautiful sandy beach. I invite you to close your eyes for a moment and transport yourself to that ideal place where you'd rather be right now.

Our perspectives on the phrase "in a better place" can indeed differ, often influenced by our individual relationships and beliefs. Working as a nurse in a hospital setting, I encounter patients with a wide range of views when it comes to dying and their perspectives on death.

Consider Patient A, who believes that he has lived a long and fulfilling life and wishes for God to end his suffering. He is convinced that the medical treatments he's receiving are causing harm to his body and stubbornly refuses them, hoping for a natural end. While these may be his heartfelt wishes, those left behind to cope with the aftermath of his passing have no choice in the matter. They must struggle with the prolonged effects and the mayhem it has caused in their lives. For them, patient A's death may not be seen as the best outcome, nor is he considered to be in a better place at that very moment.

Dealing with families of patients who are nearing the end of their lives during a hospital stay, whether prolonged or brief, where the prognosis is uncertain, can be a delicate and challenging experience. Families often beg us as healthcare providers to do everything possible to extend their loved one's life, even if the chances of recovery are only 50/50. The hope of having one last moment with their loved one drives them, and witnessing the joy on their faces when their loved one pulls through after a long and exhausting hospital stay is truly rewarding. The expressions of gratitude and heartfelt thanks can never fully convey how they feel. Many bring us tokens of appreciation, such as chocolates, cakes, and cards, just to name a few.

However, when the opposite outcome occurs, it leaves a deep ache in the pit of our stomachs and the hearts of our family members. The look on their faces when they come to realise that grief has just taken hold is heart-wrenching. There is often a unmistakable sense of tension as two families leave the hospital with contrasting narratives about the fate of their loved ones.

Some breathe a sigh of relief, while others depart with tears in their eyes. In these moments, they often express gratitude to us not for what we said, but for simply being there, providing a silent presence and support during their most challenging hours. Many times, words have failed us, and even though we've been in that situation countless times, we still can't find the words to express but rather stand in silence as they pour out their hearts to us.

Allow me to introduce you to Patient B. I distinctly remember her perspective on her situation. She expressed a deep longing, saying, "If only God could take me out of this, I wouldn't have to endure the pain I'm going through right now." During one of our conversations, she confided in me that she believed that in a better place, she would finally find relief from the relentless pain of her illness. "I will be resting pain-free, my love," she told me.

She once asked me about my belief in God, and she was surprised by my response when I told her that I do believe. We continued our conversation, and she shared her belief that God had prepared a better place for her, and it was her time to go. She made it clear that she wasn't fighting against God's plan, but she also wasn't interested in remaining in her current state; she was ready to rest. Consequently, she refused further medication, convinced that it wouldn't make a difference anymore, and she had endured enough of it.

Despite her conviction that she would find a better place in death, her family held onto a glimmer of hope that she would recover. They dreamed of taking her home for the holidays and spending it together as a family. While she had given up hope, her family's hope persisted. Sadly, she passed away a few days before Christmas, shattering her family's world.

The notion of being in a "better place" can hold varying meanings for different people. However, when someone has died, and we seek to console their friends or family members, we often use the phrase "has gone on to a better place." In many cases, this is understood as a reference to heaven.

Remember that not everyone shares the same religious beliefs or interpretations. Some people believe that their loved ones have gone directly to heaven where they watch over and protect us. Others hold the belief that the departed are in a deep sleep until the second coming of Christ.

So, before using this phrase to comfort those who are grieving, it's important to consider whether they embrace the concept of heaven in their belief system. This consideration ensures that our words offer genuine solace and resonance with the person we're trying to console.

The people around us come from diverse backgrounds, each with distinct beliefs and ideologies. Tradition, religion, and culture play significant roles in shaping our perspectives on what happens to someone's body and soul after death. Religion, in particular, influences how we embrace the notion of a "better place" in the context of a loved one's passing.

Across cultures and around the world, various religions offer distinct beliefs and viewpoints regarding life after death and the concept of being in a better place. As we explore this topic, let's closely examine some of the perspectives held by different religions.

Christianity, representing 33.1 percent of the global population, embraces the belief in the resurrection of the dead, alongside the concepts of heaven and hell. Christian teachings assert that those who have faith in Jesus Christ and adhere to His teachings will receive the gift of eternal life in the presence of God in heaven. Heaven is depicted as a realm of ultimate joy, peace, and perfect communion with God.

Those who reject God and His teachings may face eternal separation from Him in a place referred to as hell. While Christians believe in heaven, they do not believe the dead go there immediately after death. Instead, the deceased is believed to have entered a state of deep sleep until the second coming of Jesus.

Islam: Muslims believe in an afterlife comprising both paradise (Jannah) and hell (Jahannam). The righteous are expected to be rewarded with paradise, described as a place of bliss, happiness, and reward for their good deeds. Conversely, hell is regarded as a place of punishment for those who have committed evil acts and rejected the teachings of Islam.

Hinduism: Hinduism encompasses a wide array of beliefs, and views on the afterlife vary. Some Hindus adhere to the belief in reincarnation, wherein the soul is reborn into a new body after death, determined by the karma (actions) accumulated in previous lives. The ultimate aspiration is to achieve moksha (liberation) and break free from the cycle of birth and death. Others subscribe to the concept of heaven (Svarga) and hell (Naraka), where individuals are rewarded or penalised based on their actions in life.

Buddhism: Buddhists subscribe to the cycle of birth, death, and rebirth, known as samsara. They strive to attain enlightenment and break free from the cycle of suffering by adhering to the teachings of the Buddha. Nirvana, the ultimate objective, signifies a state of liberation from suffering and rebirth. It is not perceived as a place but rather a state of mind.

Judaism: throughout history, Jewish beliefs about the afterlife have evolved. Traditional Jewish views emphasise the concept of Olam Ha-Ba, the World to Come, often associated with resurrection. While Jewish Scriptures do not extensively detail the afterlife, Judaism places a greater emphasis on life in this world and fulfilling one's responsibilities to God and fellow human beings.

Sikhism: Sikhs believe in the concept of reincarnation, known as samsara, similar to Hinduism and Buddhism. The ultimate goal is to merge with God and break free from the cycle of rebirth. Sikhs aspire to attain Sach Khand, the realm of truth and divine union.

Indigenous Religions: various Indigenous religions hold unique beliefs about the afterlife. Many emphasise a deep connection with nature and ancestors, viewing the afterlife as a continuation of this world or a spiritual realm where souls dwell in peace and harmony.

Note that these descriptions offer a general overview, and beliefs within each religion can vary significantly among different sects, denominations, and individual interpretations. The perception of an afterlife as a "better place" is subjective and depends on the specific teachings and doctrines of each religious tradition.

I encourage you to contemplate if you believe in the existence of a better place for the deceased. If so, have you considered where you believe that place is? Feel free to jot down your thoughts on this statement on a piece of paper or elsewhere.

Telling those who are mourning the loss of a loved one that their beloved is in a better place may not always be beneficial or consoling. As said before, grief is a multifaceted and unique journey. Those who grieve are typically enveloped in emotions of loss, sorrow, and yearning. Hearing that their loved one is in a better place might inadvertently diminish or invalidate their grief, leading them to believe they shouldn't be struggling with the pain they are enduring.

It's important to acknowledge that not everyone shares the same belief about what happens after death. People have diverse religious, spiritual, or philosophical views, and assuming that everyone subscribes to the idea of a "better place" can dismiss their personal beliefs and values.

When someone is grieving the loss of a loved one and hears others say that their loved one is in a better place, it can evoke a range of emotions and responses. While these words are often offered with good intentions, they may not always provide comfort or solace to the grieving individual. As we support our loved ones and friends, we must allow them to recognise and accept their own emotions regarding the loss. It's okay to feel a mix of emotions, including sadness, anger, confusion, or even frustration when hearing that statement. Allow yourself and others to experience these feelings without judgement.

In every aspect of life, communication is the key, so allow the bereaved to communicate their needs to others. Having said that, they must also let those supporting them know if they find comfort in certain types of support or if specific phrases are not helpful. Openly expressing your feelings and preferences can foster better understanding and more meaningful interactions.

Grief is a deeply personal experience, and everyone finds different meanings and ways to cope. If the notion of a "better place" doesn't resonate with you, seek solace in your own beliefs, spirituality, or personal understanding of the afterlife or the continuation of the essence of your loved one. If you feel comfortable, gently educate those around you about the complexities of grief. Explain how certain statements may impact your emotions and suggest alternative ways they can provide support, such as offering a listening ear or sharing cherished memories of your loved one.

Understanding the diversity of beliefs surrounding the afterlife and respecting the grieving person's perspective is crucial in providing meaningful support during their difficult journey. As we navigate this ground of varying beliefs, our ability to empathise and offer genuine comfort can make a significant difference in helping those in grief find their own path toward healing and understanding.

POWERFUL CHAPTER TAKEAWAYS

1. Grief involves a mix of emotions, including sadness, anger, guilt, and confusion. Telling someone their loved one is in a better place may not address these complex emotions and may even lead to feelings of guilt or resentment for not feeling comforted by the statement.

2. When people lose loved ones, they often long for their physical presence and the relationship they shared. Telling them their loved one is in a better place may unintentionally undermine that sense of longing and make them feel disconnected from them.

3. Each person's grief journey is unique, and what may bring comfort to one person may not have the same effect on another. It's important to remember that grief is a highly individualised process, and there is no one-size-fits-all approach to providing comfort or solace.

4. Remember, grief is a unique and individual journey. It's essential to honour your feelings, seek support from understanding individuals, and find meaning and comfort in your own way.

5. In essence, while "They're in a better place" may be well-intentioned, it's crucial to approach this sensitive topic with respect, empathy, and a willingness to meet those grieving where they are in their journey. Your presence and genuine support can be a source of immense comfort during their time of grief.

They Lived
Their Life

When someone you love becomes a memory,
that memory becomes a treasure.
— UNKNOWN

T he phrase "They lived their life" serves as a statement or expression used to acknowledge that someone has had a complete life. It often implies that they have experienced a range of significant events, made choices, and created meaningful memories throughout their lifetime. This phrase is commonly employed to summarise or reflect on a person's life story or journey, typically after death or when assessing their impact on others.

However, regardless of a person's age at the time of passing, it evokes a profound sense of grief. Age does not diminish the pain or emotions that accompany loss. Death does not discriminate based on age; it can occur at any moment, catching us unaware. It serves as a reminder that none of us are exempt from its inevitability.

Even if someone has lived a full life, their family and loved ones may still have unfulfilled dreams or unspoken words. The reality is that readiness for such a loss is elusive; it can come abruptly and unexpectedly. Death underscores the importance of cherishing every moment we have, as it reminds us that the timing of our departure is beyond our control.

When someone dies, regardless of the age or life span, it remains a profound shock to their family. It elicits a natural response from the family: grief. Emotions are valid, and the right to grieve is unquestionable.

There's a common belief that when people reach the age of 80 and beyond, their passing is a natural event, and it's assumed they have lived life to its fullest.

During the writing of this book, I engaged in conversations with a group of friends to gather insights on the things people say to you when experiencing grief. One of the comments that emerged was, "You were very fortunate that your mother lived to the age of 92." This remark made one of my friends reflect on her grief. She shared that it almost made her feel guilty for mourning the loss of her mother when many people never had the chance to meet their own parents or experience the gift of longevity in their relationships.

She found herself compelled to conceal her grief and the pain of missing her mother from that individual. There was an unwavering feeling that she shouldn't express her sorrow because, in the eyes of this person, her mother's long and well-lived life should only warrant gratitude. The longing for her mother's presence, for conversations and shared moments, was deep-seated. It became challenging to confide in someone she considered a friend, as their perspective on her mother's passing differed significantly from her own. This difference in understanding and empathy gradually created a break in their friendship. Regardless of the age of the person who died, the void remains. The pain is not measured by the length of time you get to spend with that person.

A mother's love holds a unique and enduring place in her children's hearts, whether she became a mother in her teens or later in life. It is essential to recognise that the right to grieve the loss of a mother is not determined by the circumstances of their relationship. Love is the heartbeat of grief, and its depth is not dictated by age or life stage.

Drawing from personal experience, I lost my mother at the tender age of 53. Her passing left behind countless milestones and moments yet to be shared—birthdays, weddings, graduations, and more. The deep void she left was not lessened by my friend's mother, who experienced her loss at the golden age of 92. Our grief journeys were unique, shaped by our individual bonds with our mothers, the memories we held dear, and the futures we had envisioned.

Again, grief does not adhere to a one-size-fits-all model. It is a deeply personal experience, colored by the love and connection shared with the person we've lost. Each grief journey is as unique as the relationship it mourns. Whether a teen mother or a mature mother, the love they bestowed upon their children is immeasurable, and the right to grieve their loss is absolute.

There is no need for guilt or comparison in the world of grief. It is a course marked by its own challenges, where the intensity of sorrow is felt deeply by each individual who experiences it. All those who grieve deserve validation and understanding, regardless of their mother's age at the time of her passing.

In the uncertainty of life, grief is a thread that weaves through the human experience. It reminds us of the profound love we have shared, the bonds that endure even in our absence, and the strength we summon to carry on. Let us remember that grief, like love, knows no bounds or conditions, and every heartache is a testament to the significance of the love we hold for those we have lost.

In recent months and years, my family has experienced a series of losses, prompting reflection on the diverse ages at which our loved ones passed. These ages spanned from just a few hours to a remarkable 102 years old. Each individual left a unique mark on our lives.

I think of the baby who departed just a few hours after birthing whose time on this earth was tragically brief, robbed of the opportunity to experience life's joys or a parents' love. It's heart-wrenching to imagine this infant never had the chance to leave the hospital, wear the beautiful clothes chosen by her parents, or experience sleepless nights and tender moments in the nursery.

The pain and sorrow new parents endure in such situations are unimaginable. Their grief is profound, their hearts aching for the life that could have been. How do you explain this to a grieving heart? A moment meant to be remarkable turned painfully bitter. It wasn't the moment the family had planned for; it wasn't the ending they were expecting.

These parents had already formed a bond with their child during nine months of anticipation and preparation. They had dreams, hopes, and plans for a future together that were suddenly shattered. The nursery they lovingly decorated remained untouched, a reminder of the life they had envisioned but would never live.

As friends and family, let us approach grief with sensitivity and empathy. In moments like these, words cannot erase the pain, but our presence and understanding can provide comfort. We must allow them to mourn their loss, validate their feelings, and offer unwavering support during this heart-wrenching time.

Reflecting on the various ages at which our loved ones passed, it becomes evident that each life, regardless of duration, holds significance and impact. The depth of grief is not measured by years lived but by the love and connections formed during that time.

The loss of life due to gun violence is a tragedy that leaves families with an indescribable void, as they never had the chance to say their goodbyes. They are left waiting for answers that may never come, dealing with the pain of an unexpected and senseless loss.

I vividly recall the heart-wrenching phone call that delivered the devastating news about our 17-year-old cousin. She found herself in the wrong place at the wrong time, becoming a victim of a random act of gun violence. Her life was tragically cut short, and her family's world was shattered with that phone call. Plans for the morning and the night, dreams of her upcoming 18th birthday celebration, thoughts of the university she would attend, and visions of her walking down the aisle—all abruptly halted. Her parents would never witness these milestones or experience the joy of grandchildren. What amplifies this loss is that she was an only child.

While well-meaning individuals may attempt to offer comfort by remarking that she lived her life to the fullest, her parents are left with an irreplaceable void. Something essential is missing, and life will never be the same. The dreams she harboured for her future, her aspirations for her dream job, and the adventures she had planned—all came to a tragic and untimely end.

It's crucial to recognise that in matters of grief and loss, what we perceive as a well-lived life may not align with the perspective of those who are grieving. Sometimes, our choice of words, though well-intentioned, may not provide the intended comfort. I often reflected on my great granduncle who passed away at the remarkable age of 102, believing he had lived a fulfilling life. However, I've come to understand that I can never truly know if he achieved all that he set out to accomplish. Did he fulfil his dreams of owning a house, starting a family, obtaining a car, or pursuing education? It's a question that remains unanswered, but what is certain is that the pain we felt upon his passing was no less profound than the loss of any other family member.

Reflecting on the loss of my sister, Curliana, who departed at the tender age of 23, I find myself contemplating the life she never had the chance to experience. She missed witnessing her children's growth—those first steps and first words that every parent cherishes. At the time of her passing, her youngest, Jerbarry, was merely six months old; now, he's in the second grade. She never had the opportunity to celebrate her children's birthdays or witness their first days of school. Motherhood remained a dream unfulfilled, and she wouldn't be there to see her daughter, Abney, sit for his secondary school entrance exams. There were no school graduations, and no family photos, and we dearly miss celebrating her birthdays and many other cherished moments we used to share.

Life can indeed feel profoundly unfair, particularly to those who have experienced the loss of a loved one. Grief often causes survivors to perceive death as a thief, one that steals away the simple joys and happiness that life can offer. The perception of what equals a well-lived life can vary significantly from one person to another, making it a deeply personal and complex matter.

What we may regard as a well-lived life, filled with achievements, possessions, or milestones, might be entirely different for someone else. The meaning of a well-lived life go beyond material gains and societal expectations, probing into the realm of emotions, connections, and personal experiences.

Certain moments can trigger unresolved grief, particularly when a spouse passes away. These instances can cast a long shadow over the survivor's ability to embrace life, especially activities they once enjoyed together. The surviving spouse may withdraw into self-imposed isolation, wrestling with a deep sense of emptiness and reluctance to engage in activities once shared with a partner.

One moving story comes to mind about a couple who received an invitation to a grand 50th wedding anniversary banquet. The invitation was extended to them and their group of friends, all celebrating their half-century milestones together. However, the husband felt unable to attend such a joyous occasion without his wife. It was a celebration they had imagined together, every aspect intertwined with cherished memories of their life as a couple.

The mere thought of attending alone weighed heavily on his heart, feeling like a betrayal of the unity and togetherness that had defined their marriage. How could he partake in the festivities without the one who had been his companion on life's journey for five decades? The solitude seemed unbearable, reminding him of his loss.

As he contemplated the invitation, guilt consumed him. It wasn't a matter of not wanting to honour his dear friends' golden years; rather, it was a deeply personal struggle to reconcile past joy with present sorrow. To attend would mean facing a reality where his spouse would forever be absent, standing alone amidst couples rejoicing in their enduring love stories.

In this emotional moment, we look at the complexities of grief and its profound impact on one's ability to engage with the world. It serves as a reminder that healing is not a linear path, and sometimes, even amid celebrations, the weight of absence can be too heavy to bear.

As we delve into the story of this husband's dilemma, we are prompted to reflect on the difficult emotions that accompany loss and the resilience required to navigate a world forever altered by the absence of a beloved partner.

Continuing with the theme of "They Lived Their Life," we explore deeper into the story of this husband, who, like so many others, face with the challenge of living a life permanently changed by grief.

For months, he has been suffering over his decision, witnessing his friends' excitement as they prepared for the grand celebration. They shared memories and stories from five decades of marriage—a journey he had shared with his wife, but now, faced alone.

Within the confines of his home, he confronted daily reminders of their shared life—the empty chair at the dining table, her favourite books neatly lined on the shelf, and the familiar routines they once enjoyed together. However, these activities now lacked their former attraction. He couldn't bring himself to visit their cherished restaurant, embark on their favourite hikes, or attend gatherings where couples danced and laughed in each other's embrace.

Yet, amid his solitude, a subtle transformation began to unfold. He gradually realised that while his beloved wife was physically absent, her presence lingered in the memories they had forged and the love that had sustained them for fifty years. In quiet moments, he could almost hear her voice, offering words of encouragement, laughter, and comfort.

He chose to honour their journey in his own way, opting not to attend the grand celebration but instead dedicating himself to a different kind of tribute. He poured his energy into preserving the memories of their life together, creating a scrapbook filled with photographs, mementos, and handwritten notes that captured the essence of their love story. Each page was a testament to the beauty of their shared moments, serving as a visual reminder that their love had not faded with her passing.

As he turned the pages of the scrapbook, he found comfort in the realisation that he could still celebrate their life together, not by erasing her absence but by acknowledging the profound impact she had on his existence. It was a tribute to the enduring love that transcended the boundaries of life and death.

In the end, he may not have joined his friends at the 50th wedding anniversary banquet, but he had embarked on a journey of healing and remembrance. Through the lens of his story, we see that grief does not always lead to isolation; rather, it can be a reagent for a profound reconnection with the memories and love that continue to shape our lives, even in the absence of those we hold most dear. It shows the enduring power of love.

Certainly, even if our loved ones lived their lives to the fullest, their absence leaves an undeniable void. The completeness of a life cannot be definitively measured upon its end. Each person's journey is distinct, shaped by their own joys, sorrows, and experiences that affect them in ways we may never entirely grasp.

Let us mourn our loved ones with care and sensitivity. The process of contending with a loved one's passing is deeply personal and unfolds at its own pace. Each family and individual navigate this journey uniquely, finding solace and understanding in their own manner.

There is no "right" or "wrong" way to grieve. It encompasses a broad spectrum of emotions, ranging from sadness and anger to moments of laughter and cherished memories. As outsiders offering support, we must tread lightly, extending our assistance without judgement, and allowing our grieving loved ones the freedom to grieve on their own terms.

As mentioned earlier, the way we communicate and engage with those who are mourning is crucial. Words possess the power to heal or harm, to provide comfort or induce distress. Instead of imposing our own expectations or judgements, we can simply offer a listening ear, hold space for their emotions, and provide a comforting presence.

While we may never fully comprehend the depth of another person's grief, we can serve as a source of strength and comfort by acknowledging the profound impact their loved ones had on their lives. By demonstrating our unwavering support, we show that we are here to aid them in their unique journey of remembrance and healing.

In the end, it's not about finding the perfect words to say; it's about being present, empathetic, and patient as our loved ones navigate the complex terrain of grief.

At life's end, each of us weaves a unique thread, leaving behind a legacy of experiences, connections, and memories. As we explore the stories of those who have lived their lives and faced the depths of grief, we come to understand that grief is not an ending but a continuation of the love that once bound us.

Now, let's consider cases of sudden or premature death. It can be challenging to use the phrase "They have lived their life" in the same way it might be used for someone who lived to an older age or experienced a full range of life events. When people die unexpectedly or at a young age, it may feel unjust to suggest that they have had the opportunity to fully live their lives in the conventional sense. The phrase "They have lived their life" can take on a different meaning in these circumstances. It can serve as a reminder to appreciate the moments we have, regardless of their duration, and to honour the experiences and connections our loved ones had during their time on Earth. It may not connote a lengthy or conventional life journey, but it still acknowledges the value and significance of the life that was lived.

Moreover, employing such a phrase can provide comfort and solace to those left behind, as it emphasises the importance of cherishing each day and living life to the fullest, even in the face of uncertainty and sudden loss. It reminds us that every life, regardless of its length, has an impact and a story worth acknowledging and remembering.

Certainly, in the context of sudden or premature death, it's important to recognise that the phrase "they have lived their life" can be seen as a way to express condolences and empathy. It acknowledges the person's existence and the experiences they had up to that point, no matter how brief or unexpected their journey may have been. It's also a reminder that life, regardless of its duration, is precious and should not be taken for granted. Sudden loss can be a bleak reminder of the fragility of life and the importance of making the most of the time we have.

In such situations, the focus often shifts from the quantity of life to the quality of life. It becomes an opportunity to celebrate the moments of joy, love, and connection that the person experienced and shared with others. It encourages us to reflect on the impact that even a short life can have on those it touches.

Ultimately, whether the phrase is used to reflect on a long, full life or a life cut tragically short, it is a way to honour and remember the individual and their unique journey, while also prompting us to consider how we can make the most of our own lives and the time we have with our loved ones. Thus, there are moments when the phrase may not be well received by the griever.

The phrase "They lived their life" can sometimes have a negative impact when used insensitively or inappropriately, especially in situations of loss or adversity. Knowing when and how to use such phrases is very important. Here are some scenarios where this phrase might be received negatively:

- **Insensitive Remarks:** if we offer condolences by saying "Well, at least they lived their life" to someone who has experienced a significant loss, it can come across as callous or lacking empathy, minimizing the depth of the person's grief.

- **Premature Closure:** in some instances, using this phrase can give the impression that the person's life and experiences are being prematurely closed or summed up, especially if their death was sudden or tragic. It may imply a sense of finality or closure that may not align with the ongoing grief and pain that loved ones are experiencing.

- **Comparison:** when comparing the life of the deceased to others, saying "They lived their life" can imply judgement or evaluation, suggesting that the person's life was somehow less meaningful or complete compared to someone else's. This can be hurtful and divisive.

- **Disregarding Circumstances:** in cases of untimely death, where a person's life was cut short due to external factors or circumstances beyond their control, the phrase might seem dismissive of the tragedy of the situation and the potential the person had for a longer life.

- **Lacking Sensitivity**: using the phrase without considering the feelings, beliefs, or cultural context of the bereaved can be insensitive. Different individuals and cultures have varying beliefs about what constitutes a fulfilling life, and using the phrase without understanding these variations can be problematic.

Toolkit of Meaningful Gestures

To help others to be more considerate when using the phrase "They lived their life," especially in sensitive or grief-related situations, you can offer the following advice:

- **Listen Actively:** encourage them to actively listen to those who are grieving. Pay attention to their words, emotions, and cues to better understand their perspectives and feelings.

- **Empathise**: remind them to put themselves in the shoes of the grieving individual. Encourage empathy and understanding by asking questions like, "How would you feel in their situation?"

- **Avoid Comparisons**: emphasise that comparisons between the deceased and others should be avoided. Each person's life is unique and should not be judged or evaluated in relation to someone else's.

- **Be Mindful of Timing**: stress the importance of considering the timing of using this phrase. In the immediate aftermath of a loss, it might be best to focus on offering condolences and support, rather than making statements about the life lived.

- **Ask for Permission**: suggest that if they are unsure whether to use the phrase, they can ask the grieving individual if it's appropriate to discuss the life and memories of the deceased. This respects the grieving person's preferences.

- **Consider Cultural Differences***: remind them to be sensitive to cultural differences and beliefs surrounding death and the afterlife. What is seen as appropriate or meaningful can vary widely among cultures and religions.

- **Offer Support**: encourage them to be supportive and available to listen without judgement. Sometimes, simply being there for someone who is grieving is more meaningful than words.

- **Use It Thoughtfully**: if they decide to use the phrase, advise them to do so thoughtfully and with a genuine intention to honour the person's life and experiences. It should be used as a way to remember and celebrate, not dismiss, or diminish.

- **Respect the Grieving Process**: remind them that grief is a process, and everyone experiences it differently. Encourage patience and understanding as the grieving individual navigates the journey.

- **Educate Themselves**: suggest that they educate themselves about grief, mourning practices, and cultural norms surrounding death. Understanding these aspects can help them communicate more sensitively.

- **Offer Practical Help**: sometimes, actions speak louder than words. Offer advice on practical ways to support the grieving person, such as helping with arrangements, cooking meals, or running errands.

By providing this guidance, you can help someone use the phrase "They lived their life" more thoughtfully and compassionately in situations where it may be relevant. It's essential to prioritise the emotional well-being of those who are grieving and show respect for their unique journey through grief.

POWERFUL CHAPTER TAKEAWAYS

Always keep in mind that every life is distinct and special to those who are mourning the loss of their loved ones.

1. Let us carry forward the understanding that grief, though it may be heavy and at times unbearably painful, is a testament to the depth of our connections and the richness of our shared experiences.

2. Different individuals and cultures have varying beliefs about what constitutes a fulfilling life, and using the phrase without understanding these variations can be problematic.

3. Remember to avoid comparing the life of the deceased to others. Saying "They lived their life" can imply judgement or evaluation, suggesting that the person's life was somehow less meaningful or complete compared to someone else's. This can be hurtful and divisive.

4. Always remember your present and listening ear can provide a more meaningful sense of support than expressing words that may come across as dismissive.

CHAPTER 5

Be Strong

Tears shed for another person are not a sign of weakness.
They are the sign of a pure heart.
— **JOSIE N. HARRIS**

G rief has a language of its own, a silent imbalance of emotions, memories, and aching hearts. In this journey through the valleys of sorrow, we encounter a phrase that has become both a well-intentioned quote and a silent burden: "Be strong." But what does it truly mean to be strong in the face of grief? Does it imply an unyielding resilience that masks our pain? Or is there a more profound strength to be discovered beneath the surface, one that embraces vulnerability, compassion, and the messy complexity of human emotions?

As I try to explore the saying "Be strong" in the context of grief and loss, let's peel back the layers to reveal a deeper truth. Discover that strength is not about denying our grief but acknowledging it. It's not about concealing our tears but letting them flow. It's not about shouldering the weight alone but seeking support and connection.

The grief journey is marked by highs and lows, moments of resilience, and times of fragility. We will explore how the well-intentioned words "Be strong" can take on new meaning when seen through the lens of compassion and self-care.

Together, we will redefine strength in the face of grief and loss, honour the memory of those we've lost, and find relief in the understanding that vulnerability is not weakness and true strength lies in the courage to grieve openly and authentically.

Strength, within the context of grief, often defies conventional definitions. It's not about being immune or invulnerable; rather, it's a remarkable form of courage. It entails facing the most painful thoughts, emotions, and memories head-on, even when they are overwhelming. It's about looking at them and saying, "You are a part of me now, and I will acknowledge you."

In the midst of grief, many find themselves wearing a mask when they interact with the outside world. On the surface, they may project an image of being "fine" while silently battling with inner turmoil. It's in this inner struggle that true strength emerges, though it may go unnoticed by others because these moments are deeply personal and often private.

Strength in grief manifests in the seemingly small yet profoundly brave acts we undertake every day. It's summoning the will to get out of bed and navigate a world that suddenly feels unfamiliar and filled with sharp edges.

It's mustering the courage to open Pandora's box of memories, fully aware that tears will flow. It's the moment you dare to speak your loved one's name out loud in public, casually, for the first time. Strength in grief is about acknowledging, experiencing, and expressing your emotions without reservation.

To broaden our understanding of the diverse form's strength can take in the grieving process, we invite you to share what strength in grief looks and feels like to you. Please share your thoughts in your journal or just on a piece of paper or tissue if that is what you can find.

So, the next time people comment on your strength, remember that they may not understand the depth of your inner journey. Take comfort in knowing that your strength is a reflection of your resilience, a strength that is forged in the crucible of loss, and it's a profound expression of love and remembrance.

Telling the bereaved to "be strong" after they've lost a loved one is a well-intentioned sentiment, but it's important to consider the context and the individual's feelings before saying it.

Saying "be strong" might come across as dismissive or minimise the depth of someone's emotions. Grief is not something that can be overcome by sheer willpower. Therefore, implying that those who grieve must be strong might make them feel pressured to hide their emotions or pretend to be okay when they're not.

The motto echoing through the corridors of my existence during the profound loss of my mother and sister was to "be strong." It seemed, at the time, that being strong meant concealing my emotions, holding back the tears that threatened to overflow. I believed that admitting my vulnerability, and confessing to those around me that I lacked the strength to continue, was associated with weakness. In those seasons of my life, strength felt alien and distant.

In the midst of my grief, I discovered that my understanding of strength was wrong. I questioned how I could be considered strong while I was deliberately avoiding the tidal wave of emotions crashing over me. How could I claim strength when I was too paralysed by fear to confront the harsh reality of what was unfolding before my eyes?

In those moments, I realised that true strength wasn't about denying my emotions or bottling up the pain. It wasn't about wearing a mask of composure while my heart shattered into a million pieces. Instead, strength revealed itself in the courage to face the range of emotions, and to allow myself to feel the depth of my sorrow without reservation.

I came to understand that strength was found in acknowledging my vulnerability, in reaching out to others for support, and in accepting that it was okay not to have all the answers. Strength, I discovered, was not about standing tall and unshaken; it was about bending under the weight of grief and finding the courage to rise again.

In the acceptance of my own fragility, I found a different kind of strength — a strength that was authentic, raw, and very human. It was in embracing my pain, in allowing the tears to flow freely, that I discovered a resilience I never knew I possessed. I learned that true strength lies in the willingness to confront our emotions, accept our limitations, and find solace in the presence of those who understand that being strong doesn't mean we have to bear the weight of our grief alone.

I found myself trapped in the expectation of being strong, but this expectation was not mine; it belonged to the world around me. People anticipated my resilience, urging me to hold it together in the face of unbearable loss. However, they didn't understand I needed to feel the depth of that great loss. I needed to allow the pain to surface, to release the heavy burden weighing me down.

Trying to be strong for others had unintended consequences. It painted a false picture of composure, making others believe I had it all under control. In doing so, I inadvertently deprived myself of the support I so desperately needed. The pressure to wear a mask of strength prevented me from acknowledging the true extent of my grief.

Being asked to be strong for everyone else became a lonely battle. While I was expected to stand firm, no one seemed strong enough to hold me up in return. It became evident that putting on this facade was perilous. It acted as a shield, yes, but it was a shield against my true emotions and genuine feelings. It prevented me from confronting the rawness of my sorrow and embracing the healing power of vulnerability.

I realised that genuine strength in grief lay in the quiet moments when I willed myself out of bed, facing the day despite the desire to hide away. It was in the solitude of my tears, unseen by others, that I confronted the reality of my pain. Real strength emerged when I began to own my feelings, allowing the waves of grief to wash over me without restraint.

True strength was not found in the comforting pats on the shoulder or whispered encouragement to be strong. Instead, it surfaced when I acknowledged my vulnerability, faced my emotions head-on, and allowed myself the space to mourn without judgement or expectations. It was in these moments of authenticity that I discovered resilience far more powerful than any facade could ever be.

One of the most hurtful moments during my grieving process occurred at the funeral service when someone approached me and uttered these words: "Be strong for your mother." It felt like a demand to suppress my pain as if displaying emotions was unacceptable. It was as though they were instructing me to shield my tears and struggles from the prying eyes of onlookers. It reminded me of the touching statement I had read in an online article that strength in grief is akin to bravery, but it feels like the opposite. It's about deliberately confronting the wounds, acknowledging the painful thoughts, emotions, and memories, and claiming them as a part of your being.

When others expect us to be strong, there is an underlying pressure to uphold an outward appearance of composure. It creates the illusion that everything is fine, that the struggle doesn't exist. These well-intentioned but misguided encouragements echo phrases we've heard too many times, promising a return to normalcy that may never arrive. The burden of being strong, not just for us but also for our families, becomes an impossible task. Society demands it of us, urging us to accomplish the unachievable. But when we falter, we shouldn't feel guilty; being strong in the face of such personal loss is not a choice.

As I reflected on the contrast between my experiences with my sister's passing and my mother's, I noticed a marked difference in the way I coped with grief.

When my sister, Curliana, passed away, I found strength within my support network, especially my mother. Despite the emotional turmoil, I understood the depth of our grief was determined by our relationship with my sister. However, some people assumed that my grief for Curliana was somehow less significant than my mother's, simply because Curliana was her daughter. This misconception overlooked the individuality of grief; we all experience it differently, irrespective of our connections.

As the firstborn, I was expected to be the pillar of strength for the family, supporting my mother during her loss. I understood the rationale behind it at the time, but we were both grieving that loss. In the eyes of others, my mother was the one hurting the most because she gave birth to my sister. She nurtured and cared for her from birth until her passing. Their bond was seen in a different light. Therefore, I was the one who needed to be strong for the others.

My own needs and grief were often overlooked as I navigated this role. I had to be brave in the face of my sorrow, all the while concealing my pain to be the source of strength for everyone. However, when my mother passed away, the dynamics shifted drastically. I found myself merely going through the motions, dealing with the practical aspects of managing family affairs. The responsibilities that my mother once assumed after my sister's death now weighed heavily on me.

Wearing the mask of bravery became a tiring battle. Being strong without showing any visible pain became an overwhelming challenge that only I knew about. The expectation to maintain composure while concealing my deep sorrow became an unbearable burden. Although well-wishers encouraged me to stay strong, in the face of losing a loved one, strength always wavers, leaving nothing but the pretence of being strong.

While the intention behind praising someone's strength during grief is often genuine, it can sometimes miss the mark. In reality, those who are grieving may feel anything but strong. Such compliments, meant to uplift, can unintentionally make them feel patronised, misunderstood, or even pressured to suppress their emotions.

The problem stems from the confusion surrounding the role of emotion in grief and the perception of what it means to be strong. Many people imagine strength as resistance, similar to a knight in dense armour, unaffected by the onslaught of painful thoughts and emotions. However, the truth is much more complex. We are not knights; we are vulnerable beings. Genuine strength in grief does not come from avoidance but from confronting the pain directly, embracing vulnerability, and allowing the waves of grief to wash over us without fear. Therefore, the most meaningful support we can offer to those grieving is not to expect them to be strong in the conventional sense. Rather, it's to acknowledge their vulnerability, to provide a safe space where they can express their emotions without judgement, and to extend compassion and understanding.

In these moments of genuine connection, true strength is found, not in resisting grief, but in bravely enduring it in all its rawness and complexity. It's through this acknowledgment of our vulnerability that we discover the immense courage residing within each of us, allowing us to navigate the stormy waters of grief with resilience and authenticity.

As we continue to explore the statement "Be strong," there are different facts within society and culture that affect or influence such phrases during grief and loss. This underscores the need for a more nuanced and compassionate approach to a deeply personal experience.

Cultural norms, as we've discussed, can vary widely. In some cultures, stoicism may be valued, while in others, open expressions of grief may be encouraged. Understanding and respecting these cultural differences is crucial in providing meaningful support to grieving individuals.

Historical context reminds us that societal attitudes toward grief have evolved over time. While past generations may have embraced public mourning, today's expectations lean toward a more private grieving process. However, this shift doesn't diminish the intensity of grief or the need for empathy and understanding.

Gender roles, deeply ingrained in society, can exert significant pressure on those who conform to stereotypes. Men may feel compelled to appear stoic, while women may feel the burden of being expected to provide emotional support. Challenging these gender norms and allowing everyone the space to grieve authentically is an important step to promoting healthier grieving processes.

Media and popular culture's portrayal of strength in the face of tragedy can create unrealistic expectations. Real-life grief rarely aligns with Hollywood scripts. The bereaved need not emulate fictional characters. Instead, they should be encouraged to express their emotions in their own way and at their own pace.

In today's age of social media where personal lives are often on display, social comparison can intensify the pressure to be strong. We must remember that behind every online persona lies a complex and unique human experience. Comparing one's grief journey to others' highlights the need for self-compassion and understanding there is no right or wrong way to grieve.

Finally, the role of support systems cannot be overstated. Friends, family, and communities play a vital part in helping us navigate our grief. Those who create a safe space for emotional expression offer invaluable support, while those expecting strength may unintentionally hinder the healing process. Encouraging open conversations and active listening within these support systems can make a world of difference.

Recognising and appreciating the intricacies of societal influence on grief allows us to approach this delicate subject with greater empathy and understanding. It underscores the importance of embracing diversity in grief responses, challenging gender stereotypes, and promoting open dialogue within our communities. By doing so, we create a more compassionate and supportive society where we can mourn, heal, and find strength in our unique and authentic ways.

As we continue to explore the theme "Be strong" in the context of grief and loss, religion serves as a guide, offering comfort and strength amidst deep sorrow. In the face of loss, the core principle of many religious beliefs is the hope of reunion with loved ones in the afterlife. This hope becomes a beacon, illuminating the path through the darkest days of mourning. It isn't just a mere wish; it's a fundamental belief that lends immense courage.

Faith in a higher power fosters trust in a divine plan. It reassures grieving hearts that loss, as inexplicable and painful as it is, is part of a greater purpose. In these moments of vulnerability, people often find the strength to be strong because of their trust in God. The belief that He is watching over, guiding, and eventually reuniting them with their loved ones provides immense comfort.

The Bible has a wellspring of verses that reinforce this faith. Passages like Psalm 34:18, "The Lord is close to the broken-hearted and saves those who are crushed in spirit," serve as a balm to the grieving soul. Such words echo the promise of divine presence in times of sadness, encouraging us to find strength in our faith.

Moreover, the Scriptures offer narratives of individuals who faced unimaginable trials and emerged stronger due to their unwavering faith. The story of Job, for instance, illustrates endurance and resilience in the face of immense suffering. Job's steadfast faith, even in the depths of his despair, is a testament to the strength that can be found through trust in God.

Religion essentially takes the phrase "Be strong" from being a simple cliché to becoming a deep belief. It represents the idea that strength is not just a human quality, but a divine blessing given to those who have faith in God. The belief that this world is only temporary and there will be a joyful reunion in the spiritual realm fills those living in the shadows of grief with hope and courage.

As we delve further into this understanding, it is clear to thank you for your leadership and support throughout this journey. Your guidance has been invaluable, and I'm grateful to have you leading our team. Looking forward to continuing our success together. Have a wonderful day!" religious beliefs not only offer a source of strength but also a framework for making sense of the inexplicable. The expression "Be strong" gains depth, becoming a spiritual call to trust, endure, and eventually, find peace amidst the profound pain of loss.

While religion offers comfort and strength to many during times of grief, it can also inadvertently cause additional pain to those who are grieving. Here are a few reasons why:

Some religious teachings emphasise the importance of enduring suffering with patience and fortitude. While this can be a source of strength, it may also create pressure for grieving individuals to suppress their natural emotions of grief, sadness, and anger. The attempt to be strong in the face of such intense emotions can lead to feelings of guilt or inadequacy.

In some religions, people might question their faith or feel guilty for not being able to handle their sorrow better. The pressure to be strong can exacerbate these feelings, making the grieving process even more complex.

Some individuals might fear that expressing their pain and questioning their faith during grief could be perceived as a lack of trust in God or divine displeasure. This fear might prevent them from seeking help or expressing their true emotions, causing them to suffer in silence.

Within religious communities, there can be judgement or misunderstanding regarding the grieving process. If individuals appear visibly distressed or openly express pain, others might question their faith or suggest that their grief is a sign of weak faith.

Those with religious beliefs often struggle with the concept of divine plans and the reasons behind human suffering. When faced with the loss of a loved one, people might struggle with questions such as "Why did God allow this?" or "What is the purpose behind this suffering?" The pressure to be strong can prevent them from exploring these questions openly, hindering their ability to find spiritual peace and understanding.

Balancing the strength found in faith with the natural, sometimes overwhelming, emotions of grief can be challenging. Hence, religious leaders and fellow believers should offer not just spiritual support but also space for honest, vulnerable conversations. Acknowledging the pain, doubts, and questions without judgement can help those who are grieving navigate their spiritual and emotional journeys.

As we console those who mourn, it is clear that a generic approach, represented by the phrase "Be strong," is neither compassionate nor wise. Grief is complex and requires acknowledgment, understanding, and empathy. Grievers should be able to mourn without judgement, express their sorrow freely, and know that their emotions are valid, regardless of societal expectations.

Let us remember this knowledge as we interact with grievers, offering understanding rather than burdening them with expectations. May our words bring comfort, enabling the bereaved to find strength in their vulnerability, resilience in their authenticity, and healing through genuine compassion.

Toolkit of Meaningful Gestures

Instead of telling someone to be strong, it's often more meaningful to offer your support and express your willingness to listen if they want to talk. You can say:

- "I'm here for you if you want to talk or if you just need someone to be with."

- "I can't imagine what you're going through, but I'm here to support you in any way I can."

- "Take all the time you need to grieve and remember that it's okay to feel a wide range of emotions."

- "I'm sending you love and strength as you navigate through this difficult time."

Ultimately, showing empathy, compassion, and being available without putting pressure on the person to be strong can be more helpful and comforting to someone who is grieving.

POWERFUL CHAPTER TAKEAWAYS

1. Always remember, the bereaved might feel anything but strong, which can make them perceive comments about their strength as hollow attempts at comfort.

2. Statements such as "Be strong" may inadvertently imply that stoicism is the preferred response, leading people to question their own emotional expressions and feel guilty for not displaying enough grief.

3. Praising their strength might unintentionally convey the expectation that suppressing emotions is the ideal, fostering a belief that being vulnerable is disappointing.

4. "You have to be strong" can sound like a threat, subtly implying consequences if one doesn't hold emotions together, adding pressure to an already overwhelming experience.

5. Most importantly, never assume someone has it together as this might prevent others from offering the compassion and support needed, inadvertently isolating them in their pain.

6. True support lies not in expecting strength, but in embracing vulnerability, providing a safe space for emotional expression, and offering unconditional compassion.

7. By acknowledging the multifaceted nature of grief, we can create a more empathetic environment, allowing individuals to navigate their grief journey with authenticity and acceptance.

C H A P T E R   6

It's Time to Move On or Get Over It

They say time heals all wounds,
but that presumes the source of grief is finite.
— **CASSANDRA CLARE**

Sitting quietly on the floor of my mom's bedroom, I decided to check out her closet and go through her clothes. As I picked up each dress, I felt a strong attachment to them. They held significance for her, and at that moment, they held even more meaning for me than I could have imagined. Memories of occasions, when she wore them, began to flood my mind, bringing her presence almost to life. Even though people expected me to let go of my memories of her, I found it incredibly difficult, especially when I held her dresses in my hands. Giving her clothes away was a tremendous challenge because I wasn't ready to say goodbye or move on.

So, what did I do? I packed some of her dresses in my suitcase to take home with me to the UK. These dresses were more than just garments to me; they were like pieces of my mother that I could keep close. Each dress held stories of laughter, shared secrets, and the genuine love between a mother and her child. Letting go felt like losing a part of her, so I chose to hold onto her dresses.

Even though it might not make sense to everyone, I wanted to keep her memory alive. So, those dresses now have a place in my closet. They're not just old clothes; they're special reminders of the woman my mom was. It's my way of preserving her spirit, as if she's still with me, even if it's just through these pieces of fabric. I was not just taking clothes home; I was taking a bit of her love and warmth with me. Each time I put on one of her dresses, I feel close to her, and instead of crying, I sometimes smile, knowing what she would say as she looked at me in her dress.

As I fight with the ongoing challenge of moving on from my grief, the realisation hits me hard: this incredible woman was once my mother. The pain of losing her isn't a fleeting emotion; it's a constant companion, a quiet ache that lingers in the depths of my heart. Moving on from grief is a task that many of us, as survivors of loss, struggle with on a daily basis.

It's not about forgetting or pretending that the pain doesn't exist. No, the process of moving on is more complex. It involves learning to coexist with the void left by her absence and acknowledging the reality of her departure while finding ways to navigate the world without her physical presence. It's understanding that the pain isn't something we overcome but something we learn to carry.

The path to move on from grief is slow and uneven. It's marked by moments of strength and resilience, as well as times of vulnerability and tears. Each step forward can feel like a massive achievement, while setbacks can be disheartening. It's a journey that requires patience, self-compassion, and the acceptance that the pain of loss will always be a part of our story.

Moving on doesn't mean severing ties with the memories or dismissing the impact our loved ones had on our lives. Instead, it's about finding a way to integrate their memories into our present, allowing them to shape our future in a positive and meaningful way. It's embracing the bittersweet beauty of reminiscing about shared moments, even if they bring tears. It's understanding that the love we have for them go beyond the physical realm.

For grief survivors, the process of moving on is not a linear one; it's a series of loops and spirals. Some days may feel like a step backward, while others bring a semblance of peace. It's about learning to coexist with the void, finding comfort in the memories, and gradually allowing the pain to transform into a touching reminder of the enduring love we shared. So, as I navigate this journey, I hold onto the understanding that moving on doesn't mean leaving my mother behind; it means carrying her with me in a different way, finding a new balance in the ever-evolving landscape of grief. It is easy to say it's time to move on when you haven't experienced the intense emotion of grief.

"It's time to move on" in the context of grief and loss can suggest that it's time for the grieving individual to begin the process of adapting to life without the person who has died. This phrase is often used with good intentions, encouraging people to start rebuilding their lives, reengage with their routines, and find ways to cope with their emotions. However, as mentioned before, it's important to recognise that the grieving process is highly personal and varies from person to person. Some individuals may be ready to make gradual changes and move forward relatively soon after the loss, while others may need more time to come to terms with their emotions and adjust to their new reality.

Saying "It's time to move on" can be supportive when spoken gently and with empathy, acknowledging the pain of those grieving and respecting their unique timeline for healing. On the other hand, it can be harmful if used insensitively, implying that the grieving person should simply "get over" the loss, which is not a realistic or compassionate expectation.

Elisabeth Kübler-Ross beautifully captured the essence of the statement, "It's time to move on or get over it" in her writing. She profoundly expressed, "The truth is, you will grieve endlessly. You won't 'get over' the loss of a loved one; instead, you will learn to coexist with it. You will heal, and you will reconstruct yourself around the void you have experienced. You will become whole again, but you will never be identical. Nor should you be unchanged, nor would you desire to be." (Grief and Grieving)

The inescapable reality of death ensures that grief is an integral part of the human experience, woven into the very fabric of our existence. Every living being automatically qualifies for the emotions of grief. It's a universal, innate response to loss, an acknowledgment of the deep connections we form, and the profound impact certain individuals have on our lives.

Moving on from grief, many would argue, is an almost impossible task. Grief isn't a hurdle to be overcome but a process to be lived through. It lingers within us, shaping our thoughts, our memories, and even our future interactions. The depth of our sorrow is a testament to the depth of our love, and our hearts are basically designed to accommodate this complex emotion.

In the face of loss, we are compelled to confront our vulnerability and the transient nature of life. Grief is not a sign of weakness; it's a mark of our capacity to love deeply and to form meaningful connections. The human heart, resilient as it is, bears the weight of grief, reminding us of those unique threads of emotions that make us human.

Rather than something to be cast aside, grief becomes a part of our story. It shapes our empathy, our understanding of others' pain, and our appreciation for the fleeting beauty of the moments we share with loved ones. Our ability to grieve and carry on despite the pain showcases the extraordinary strength inherent in the human spirit.

So, while the unmovable nature of grief is an undeniable truth, it also serves as a reminder of our shared humanity. It connects us all, reminding us of the preciousness of life, the significance of love, and the enduring power of the human heart. Grief is an enduring struggle; there is no "moving on" from it in the conventional sense. Instead, it becomes a daily battle to find the strength to be present in the life we must continue to live. At times, a survivor of grief may struggle to see the purpose in carrying on. It demands an extraordinary amount of courage and strength to confront each day, but it's a journey that must be undertaken, often driven by the awareness that people are still depending on you.

My niece's words hit me gently, but with a touching awakening after the passing of my mom—"You are now granny, aunty, and mother to us." The weight of those roles, which including love and responsibility, became apparent. It hadn't fully registered until that moment, but her words brought the stark reality home. This little girl, having lost both her mother and grandmother in a short span, now looked to me for guidance, love, and maternal care.

Motivated by a deep desire to move on and heal, I initially approached the process with a sense of urgency. I believed that by doing so, I could play those important roles for my family. However, I soon realised that the harder I tried to hasten the healing, the more challenging it became. The strain on my relationships with my loved ones was noticeable, and the disconnection grew.

What I've come to understand now is that the journey through grief is a collective one. It's not a lonely path but a shared experience that binds us together as a family. Rushing the process is not an option as grief doesn't adhere to a fast-forward button. It requires time, patience, and a shared commitment to healing.

As a family, we're learning to navigate this uncharted territory together. We're allowing ourselves the space to grieve, to feel the pain, and to support each other through the highs and lows. I've come to appreciate that healing is not a linear progression; it's a collaborative effort.

Instead of trying to move on independently, I've embraced the strength that comes from facing grief as a unit. We share memories, shed tears, and celebrate the legacy of our loved ones together. It's through this collective journey that we find solace, understanding, and the resilience needed to move forward.

In the midst of grief, I've learned that there's no need to rush the process. Healing is a gradual unfolding, and by approaching it together as a family, we are slowly finding our way to a place where we can fulfil the roles that life has unexpectedly bestowed upon us.

Grief is not a process that has a defined endpoint; rather, it is a part of our lives. It teaches us to endure and appreciate the beauty of each moment. Though the pain of loss may never fully disappear, it can develop into a source of strength, motivating us to live our lives with a renewed sense of purpose. We face life's challenges not because we've "moved on" from grief, but because we've learned to carry it with us. It's the new normal as one may put it after an ordeal with grief.

At the time, I felt immense pressure to heal quickly and move forward. But I had to confront the harsh reality that my beloved family members, including my mother and sister, were no longer with me in this lifetime. The real gravity of my loss only sank in after the funeral when I was alone with myself and my thoughts. I often found myself pondering, "What do I do when it's just me?" When the initial wave of support from friends and well-wishers had faded, and I was left alone amidst the shattered pieces of my life, I struggled with loneliness.

Returning to my flat in England after the burial of my loved ones, I confronted the daunting task of rebuilding my life, and it was in those lonely moments that the weight of my grief felt most overwhelming. Benjamin Allen's quote, "After the funeral and everybody's gone home, where do you go? It was like a big reception, and everyone came, but I was left with me to clean up the mess," resonated deeply with me because it summarised the isolation that often accompanies the grieving process.

The slightest triggers could send me spiralling back to that initial state of grief as if it had only just begun. Special occasions, the ones where we used to celebrate together, became particularly challenging. Birthdays were marked by a palpable absence, and Mother's Day proved even more touching and heart breaking. The weeks leading up to Mother's Day seemed to amplify the void left by my mother's absence. Everywhere I turned, from shop windows adorned with gift ideas to conversations about celebrating mothers, I was reminded that she was no longer physically present.

During these moments, I had to pause and remind myself that although she was no longer with me in the physical sense, her love and memories were still very much a part of my life. It was in these quiet, lonely reflections that I found consolation, even though they were often accompanied by silent tears. Grief is a journey marked by these touching raw moments when we must navigate the delicate balance of honouring our memories while moving forward in a world forever changed by loss.

Moving forward through grief involves finding a delicate balance that others may never fully understand. I hope that my writing can give a glimpse into what it feels like to be unable to move on from unresolved grief. We cannot simply force ourselves to forget lives that were once lived and had such a profound impact on those left to carry on. Grief is not something that can be neatly packed away or erased; instead, it is a part of who we are, shaping our perspectives and influencing every step we take. It is an ongoing journey without a set time frame, requiring immense strength and courage as we learn to navigate the world while carrying the weight of our loss. I have often heard the saying "Time heals" in relation to grief and loss, but from personal experience, I know that the painful emotion of grief cannot be measured by time. Rather, it is a life experience that becomes ingrained within our journey, an encounter with grief that shapes us.

Saying "Time will heal" when it comes to loss and grief may suggest that, with the passage of time, the intensity of emotional pain and sorrow following a loss will gradually diminish. Grieving is a natural and necessary process, and as time passes, we often find ways to cope with our feelings of loss and adjust to life without our loved ones. However, it's important to note that the idea of time healing grief doesn't mean that the pain completely disappears, or we forget about our loved ones. The sharpness of grief tends to soften, allowing us to carry on with our lives while still cherishing the memories of our loved ones.

Some may find healing and acceptance with time, while others might continue to struggle. Support from friends, family, or mental health professionals can play a crucial role in helping us navigate the grieving process.

Throughout my own experience with grief, I can confidently say that as the years pass, it becomes uncertain how your grief will manifest. The reality is that grief may persist with us until our own death. During the first year of my grief, it felt incredibly challenging. The pain I endured was unlike any other. However, as time goes on, I learn how to cope with my emotions when they resurface. I cannot predict how anyone will feel when faced with the loss and death of a loved one, but I can share with you that each year of grief is unique. It is completely normal to feel deep sadness for more than a year, and sometimes even for many years, after losing someone you love. Do not pressure yourself to feel better or move on just because others think you should.

Allow yourself the necessary time to grieve for your loved ones. Remember, this journey has no fixed endpoint; there's no race to a finishing line because there simply isn't one. Often, those around you might push for you to move on, believing it's what the departed would want. While these sentiments come from a place of care, they can inadvertently add pressure.

It's crucial to be compassionate with yourself during this process. Resist the urge to adhere to a specific timeline dictated by well-meaning but unrealistic expectations. You cannot rush healing after losing someone dear, someone who played a significant role in your life. The common phrase "Time heals all wounds" doesn't mean you'll ever truly get over the loss.

Your life has undergone a profound change, and it will never revert to what it once was when that person was alive. Embrace the natural flow of grief, allowing it the time and space it requires. It's not about moving on; it's about learning to live with the void your loved ones' absence has left behind, finding ways to incorporate their memories into your life, and, in time, discovering new normalcy that accommodates your grief.

Over the years, I've come to understand that grief is an overwhelming emotion that never truly vanishes. It's an ever-changing journey where no two days are the same. The progression through the stages of grief is a highly individual experience, and, as a friend once reminded me, there are moments when it feels like grief might consume us entirely and leave us to die. These feelings don't simply vanish overnight; they linger, and if we're not careful, they can wreak havoc in our lives.

At times, I feel like a new-born, taking those first steps, saying those initial words, and accomplishing little things that would make our loved ones proud. Navigating grief often reminds me of my mother's patience with my brother during his early years. He faced unique challenges due to a reaction to a vaccine he received as an infant. This reaction left him with a speech impairment, swallowing difficulties, and an underdeveloped arm. Feeding him felt like a lifelong endeavour, but my mother, with unwavering patience, ensured he ate every last spoonful. What might have been a simple task for other children his age took him longer, but he persisted and made progress. Reflecting on how far he has come made me realise that my mother had to find ways to cope until he could manage on his own. This, to me, encapsulates the essence of dealing with grief—finding that balance in our lives.

As I've walked this path, others have reached out to me in tears, seeking guidance on how to move forward with their grief without feeling guilty. I've received countless messages from people who have recently lost someone special, struggling to move on. It may sound harsh, but the truth is that this stage of grief is necessary for healing. When they ask where to begin,

I remind them that they will never "get over it" or "move on" from their grief. Grief is not something you can't cast aside; it's more like a birthmark that becomes an indelible part of you. Embrace it and make it a personal chapter of your story.

Trying to rush past grief or pretending it doesn't exist won't make it any easier. In reality, no one can say they've moved on from grief, but what we can say is that we've learned how to navigate it, and that makes all the difference. It's what allows us to smile on days when moving forward seems impossible, on days when we feel grief might consume us.

Personalising your emotions and avoiding comparisons with others is vital. In fact, those whom you compare yourself to are likely silently admiring your ability and strength in coping with your grief. We're not cut from the same fabric, and the same holds true for our experiences with grief. Those around you, even those who have experienced a similar level of grief, may appear to be doing better while you're taking baby steps.

I remember waking up in the same room as my siblings after the loss of our mother and sister, wondering how they could seem so cheerful as if nothing had happened. It made me question whether they cared or if they were heartless. However, as the days turned into months, I realised how wrong I was. We all come to terms with our loss at different stages and in our own time.

The appearance of being okay doesn't necessarily reflect the truth about someone's inner feelings when it comes to grief. Some are never truly okay but put on a facade because they need to show up for others in their lives. Some responsibilities cannot be neglected, and life goes on. Grief becomes a permanent resident in our lives, and we must make room for it and learn to incorporate it into our daily routines. While we may not have chosen this unwelcome guest named grief, we can choose how we coexist with it.

In my years as a healthcare professional, I've encountered a prevalent misconception among people who believe that because we work closely with those at the end of life, it should be easier for us to cope with loss. There's an assumption that our professional demeanour shields us from the same depth of grief experienced by others. Even our colleagues, especially those who haven't personally faced death, often expect us to bounce back swiftly from our own losses. It's a fine line between maintaining professionalism and acknowledging our human side beyond the uniform. Outside of our roles, we too are exposed to the same feelings and emotions as anyone else.

I vividly recall a colleague's account of feeling deeply hurt by the way she was treated when her loved one passed away. The response from those working with her was shockingly insensitive, given her position in the hospital, where she worked closely with palliative patients. Their response was dismissive, suggesting she should be accustomed to such situations. They failed to recognise that this loss was her personal tragedy, someone who held a special place in her heart.

Imagine the heart-wrenching moment of witnessing your loved one being wheeled into the hospital or receiving emergency CPR. In those panic-stricken moments, rationality eludes you, and nothing seems to make sense. The line between your professional responsibility and your role as the patient's daughter blurs. It's a situation where your knowledge and expertise momentarily feel futile as you grapple to make sense of your position and responsibilities amid the chaos.

These experiences serve as a stark reminder that healthcare professionals, just like everyone else, are not immune to the profound impact of loss. We navigate the intricate dance between our professional obligations and the deeply human emotions that come with witnessing the fragility of life, especially when it hits so close to home. Others need to acknowledge our vulnerability and offer understanding, recognising that behind the scrubs and white coats, we are people affected by the decline and flow of life and death.

Frontline workers, including police officers, firefighters, and ambulance crews, face the harsh realities of emergencies daily. They step into the chaos, often unaware that they might be attending to a family member, a colleague, or a loved one. Despite the shock of what they witness, these dedicated professionals soldier on, fulfilling their duties without hesitation. It's a testament to their resilience and commitment to the job at hand. However, it's the day after the incident that proves to be incredibly challenging.

The echoes of the past linger, especially when they recall the last moments of the person they tried to save. Moving forward during grief becomes a daunting task. The weight of those memories, the images of a life slipping away despite their best efforts, can be overwhelming. It's during this time that the profound impact of their job becomes apparent.

Yet, amid the darkness, there comes a moment when these brave souls realise those close to them believe that it's time to move on. Grief, like an unwelcome guest, has settled in their hearts, but they find the strength to confront it and make it a part of the invisible medal that dangles around their necks and hearts. They acknowledge the pain, sorrow, and haunting images, and start the arduous journey of healing. Most do this silently, afraid of the judgement that awaits in the form of comments such as "it's your job" and "You should know what to expect."

Those observing with unspoken words, which speak volumes, believe that moving on should be easy for you because of the nature of your job. As they progress on their journey with grief, this does not mean forgetting or erasing the past; instead, it's about honouring the memories while finding the courage to live beyond the shadows of grief.

Moving on during grief, especially for those on the frontline, is not a sign of weakness nor is it an easy task; it's a testament to their resilience. It's about accepting the harsh realities of their profession, acknowledging the toll it takes on their emotional well-being, and seeking the support they need to navigate the turbulent waters of loss. In finding solace and support, they discover the strength to carry on, not just as professionals but as human beings who have faced the depths of despair and emerged scarred but stronger on the other side. No one dares to see the pain in their eyes or the secret of their tears. The soldier in bravery learns to incorporate grief as part of the duty daily.

Coping with the loss of a loved one is far from simple or easy, despite how it may appear. Grief is a deeply personal experience, and those going through it often find themselves in an indescribable state. The stages of grief are not fixed, and the process doesn't follow a specific order. The nature of our relationship with the deceased greatly influences how grief is navigated.

It's essential to understand that love cannot be quantified, and consequently, we cannot dictate how people should mourn their loved ones. Each person's connection with the deceased is unique, and outsiders may not fully grasp the depth of their bond. In certain situations, the dynamics of your connection with the deceased individual can lead others to underestimate or overlook the grieving process. This is particularly common when the relationship is characterised by distance, infrequent interactions, difficulty, or estrangement, such as in the case of a divorce.

In these instances, the unexpected intensity of grief may catch you off guard, and those around you might find it challenging to understand your emotions. The lack of awareness about your relationship with the deceased person might contribute to a misunderstanding of your grieving experience.

These factors can create a sense that your grief is somehow less valid, or that your emotions should be less intense. Consequently, you might find yourself lacking the emotional support people typically receive during times of mourning. This dynamic poses unique challenges, as your perception of grief and the external understanding of your situation may not align with the conventional expectations surrounding loss.

Consider the example of an ex-spouse mourning the loss of a former partner. While society might assume the person still legally married to the deceased would grieve longer, this overlooks the connection that an ex-spouse still shares. Their relationship, though transformed, remains significant and should not be dismissed.

In a similar vein, stepparents often face such a dilemma. Grief is a universal emotion that touches all of us, regardless of our roles or positions in people's lives. It's crucial to acknowledge and respect the grief of all individuals, irrespective of their relationship status, and refrain from urging them to move on prematurely. Everyone deserves the space and understanding to mourn in their own way, honouring the unique connections they shared with the departed soul.

Recognising and honouring the depth of one's grief does not negate the idea that, in time, moving forward is a natural part of the healing process. However, moving on should be approached with sensitivity and understanding. Those grieving need the freedom to progress at their own pace, without the pressure to conform to societal expectations or arbitrary timelines.

Toolkit of Meaningful Gestures

- The intensity and duration of grief are not determined by societal norms or the perceived closeness of a relationship. Understanding and respecting that each person's grief journey is unique, regardless of the circumstances, is essential.

- Instead of trying to rush past grief, acknowledging it and making it a personal part of the story is essential. Embracing grief, rather than attempting to erase or forget, allows for a more authentic and healing experience.

- Providing and seeking support during the grieving process is crucial. Friends, family, and community play a vital role in offering encouragement, empathy, and patience. Listening without judgement and allowing space for both good and bad days is essential.

- Moving forward doesn't mean returning to the past; it involves discovering a new normal that accommodates grief. This process is gradual and individualised, guided by one's own pace and time.

- Acknowledging and validating grief experiences that may not align with societal expectations is important. Whether the relationship was distant or challenging, everyone deserves the space to mourn in their own way.

Remember, grief is a complex and multifaceted emotion. These takeaways highlight the importance of recognising it and approaching the healing process with compassion, patience, and understanding.

POWERFUL CHAPTER TAKEAWAYS

1. The grieving process is highly individual, and everyone experiences it uniquely. The nature of your relationship with the departed shapes your grief, and it's crucial to allow yourself the necessary time and space to navigate this emotional journey.

2. Moving on from grief is not a linear process; it involves a series of loops and spirals. There will be moments of strength and resilience, as well as moments of vulnerability and tears. Patience, self-compassion, and an acceptance of the enduring pain are key elements in this journey.

3. Moving on doesn't mean severing ties with memories or dismissing the impact of loved ones on our lives. It's about finding a way to integrate their memories into our present, allowing them to shape our future in a positive and meaningful way.

4. Grief is not something to be overcome; instead, it becomes a part of our lives. It teaches us endurance, resilience, and appreciation for the beauty of each moment. The pain of loss may never fully disappear, but it can transform into a source of strength.

5. Professionals in roles dealing with death and loss, such as healthcare workers and first responders, also experience profound grief. The expectation to "move on" quickly can be detrimental, and acknowledging their vulnerability is crucial for understanding and support.

CHAPTER 7

You Are Still Young

*How lucky I am to have
something that makes saying goodbye so hard.*
— WINNIE THE POOH

I n times of grief and loss, finding the right words can be challenging. People often reach for familiar phrases in an attempt to bring comfort, such as "You're still young." While these words may come from a place of kindness, they need to be approached with great sensitivity and care.

Grief doesn't discriminate based on age; its deep pain affects individuals regardless. In this exploration, we delve into the reasons why saying "You're still young" to someone grieving might not always provide the comforting reassurance it intends to.

Age doesn't shield anyone from the inevitability of death or guarantee a longer lifespan than older generations. Death doesn't adhere to an age limit; it can touch us at any stage of life. Given the unpredictability of life's tragic events, it might be unwise to assume that consoling others by saying they are still young is a wise approach. Grief is a multifaceted, intensely painful experience, and the depth of sorrow is not diminished by our age. The younger generation's encounter with grief is just as profound and their pain equally severe.

The depth of grief we experience isn't diminished by our youth. When a child loses a parent, the void left behind is just as profound, needing the same understanding and support. I vividly recall when my sister passed away; we often overlooked the children in our midst. We assumed they couldn't fully understand the life-altering event that had occurred. However, we were mistaken; they were struggling with their grief just as intensely as we were.

Can you picture waking up one day, and your mother is no longer there—her presence vanished? For children, that void is as noticeable as it is for adults. They long to feel the presence of their mothers, fathers, sisters, or any close family members. Kids comprehend more than we often give them credit for.

They, too, are trying to make sense of the immense loss, navigating the same emotions and uncertainties as adults. We must acknowledge their grief and offer them the support and understanding they need during such challenging times.

Certainly, the emotional landscape of children dealing with grief is intricate and often underestimated. Their young minds struggle with the complexities of loss, just like adults, although their understanding might be filtered through a lens of innocence and confusion.

In their honesty, children confront the absence of their loved ones with a rawness that can be both heartbreaking and enlightening. Their questions, though sometimes difficult to answer, reflect a deep need for understanding. "Where did they go?" and "Will they come back?" are inquiries that echo the depths of their longing. The absence is not just physical but also emotional, leaving them with a sense of emptiness that is hard to articulate.

Moreover, children absorb the grief-laden atmosphere around them. They observe the tears, the sombre tones, and the hushed conversations. Even if they don't fully grasp the magnitude of death, they sense the sorrow and void. This awareness can sometimes lead to confusion, anxiety, or even guilt. They might blame themselves or feel abandoned, amplifying their emotional turmoil.

As they grow, these unresolved emotions can manifest in various ways. It might affect their relationships, school performance, or overall sense of security. The above are the signs and symptoms I noticed in my niece during her season of grieving, which she is still navigating at the moment.

Hence, acknowledging grief is not just an act of compassion; it's essential for their emotional well-being and future development. Supporting grieving children involves creating a safe space for them to express their feelings, fears, and questions. It means answering their inquiries with patience and honesty, even when the answers are difficult. It also involves including them in the mourning process, allowing them to participate in rituals or ceremonies, giving them a sense of closure and understanding.

Additionally, professional guidance such as therapy or counselling can equip them to cope with their grief effectively. Through these avenues, they learn their emotions are valid, that it's okay to feel anger, sadness, or confusion, and that healing is a gradual process.

I recall a time when we were uncertain about how to navigate my niece's behaviour as she struggled with her grief. It was a confusing and challenging period for us all. Recognising the need for expert guidance, we decided to seek professional help. This decision proved to be transformative for her.

Under the guidance of a skilled counsellor, my niece's bewildering and unusual behaviours began to transform. The counsellor provided her with a safe space to express her emotions, helping her unravel the sage of grief that had enveloped her young heart. One of the tools that proved instrumental in her healing journey was a journal.

In this journal, my niece creatively mapped down her emotions. It became a rescue for her thoughts, fears, and hopes. Through the act of writing, she found a channel to express the sadness and confusion that had overwhelmed her. Each entry was a brave confrontation of the stormy emotions that accompanied her grief.

The counselling sessions and the journaling process gradually became her sanctuary, a refuge where she could confront her pain without judgement. The act of putting her feelings into words offered her a measure of control in a situation that seemed uncontrollable. It became a vital part of her healing process, enabling her to explore the depths of her grief and, in the process, find the strength to cope.

Witnessing her transformation was a touching reminder of the power of professional help and the therapeutic benefits of self-expression. Her journey, marked by the pages of that journal, became a beacon of hope for our family. It demonstrated the importance of seeking support and providing young hearts with the tools they need to navigate the intricate landscape of grief.

In essence, recognising the depth of children's grief is not just an act of kindness; it's an important step in helping them navigate their loss and emerge emotionally resilient. By acknowledging their pain and supporting them in their journey, we empower them to face life's challenges with strength and understanding, fostering a foundation for emotional well-being in their future.

I look at a scenario where a young mother experiences the loss of her child either through miscarriage, stillbirth or at any time during her child-bearing years. In the face of unimaginable loss, the response, "At least you can try again," though well-intentioned, can deepen the pain. It overlooks the complex and often agonising journey of infertility that many individuals endure.

The world is fraught with medical complications that challenge the prospect of conception. Conditions that hinder fertility are not uncommon, making the path to parenthood difficult for numerous couples. I've witnessed the resilience of friends and family members who persist, navigating the harsh terrain of treatments like IVF and egg harvesting. For some, these treatments are miracles, bestowing the gift of a longed-for child. Yet, for others, they signify heartbreak and anguish.

I remember a conversation with a close friend after her successful treatment. "Jay," she said, her voice a mix of hope and trepidation, "I just wanted the test to show positive. I don't think I could have endured another negative result." Her words carried the weight of countless miscarriages and several times her hope was dashed. Her desire was simple: to complete her family.

The pain lies not just in the loss but also in the proximity to fulfillment. To be so close, to glimpse the possibility of a family, only for it to slip away, leaves an indelible mark on the soul. Every glance at a happy family with their children becomes a distant reminder of what could have been.

In such moments, saying, "You're still young" takes on a different hue. It becomes a reminder not of the possibility of trying again but of the endurance and strength within these individuals. Despite the heartbreak, they persist. Despite the tears, they find the courage to face another day. Their youth, in this context, embodies a spirit that refuses to be broken, a tenacity that propels them forward despite the agony of their journey. However, it is vital for us, as a society, to understand that the pain of child loss and infertility doesn't dissipate with time. It is not something that can be easily replaced or forgotten.

Suggesting the bereaved can try again because they are young, should be done with empathy and understanding, acknowledging the strength it takes to keep going despite the shattered dreams. For these young mothers, the resilience they demonstrate is a testament to the enduring human spirit, reminding us of all of the depth of their courage, and the significance of acknowledging their grief with compassion.

Telling someone "You're still young" often carries an implicit sense of hope, suggesting the possibility of trying again. But in the context of infertility and repeated miscarriages, this hope can feel more like a cruel reminder of what might never be. For families struggling with the pain of infertility, every miscarriage and unharvested egg represents a medical setback, as well as a loss of potential life. These are not merely clinical failures; they are the demise of dreams, the extinguishing of the flickering hope for a child that was so desperately wanted.

Each unfulfilled pregnancy is a reminder of the many babies that could have been, the laughter that could have filled their homes, and the tiny hands that could have been held. The approach of every due date, every missed opportunity to announce a pregnancy, is a constant, aching reminder of what could have been: the birthdays that could have been celebrated, the family gatherings that could have been complete.

The void left by these losses isn't measured in merely physical terms; it's an emotional chasm. It's the missed lullabies that will never be sung, the first steps that will never be taken, and the bedtime stories that will never be shared. It's the lost opportunities to witness a child's milestones: from the first smile to the first day of school, experiences that these families yearn for, but fear might forever elude them.

This pain is not diminished by youth; it's not something that time automatically heals. Instead, it lingers, shaping the very fabric of these families' lives. Each unsuccessful attempt becomes a scar, a constant reminder of what they have been through and what they continue to endure.

Furthermore, societal expectations and well-meaning but misplaced comments can exacerbate this pain. The statement, "You're still young" can inadvertently dismiss the profound grief these families experience. It doesn't account for the countless doctor appointments, the invasive procedures, and the emotional toll of each unsuccessful attempt. It doesn't acknowledge the strength it takes to face disappointment, to muster the courage to hope again despite repeated heartbreaks.

In essence, while it is said to instill hope, it often fails to recognise the depth of the sorrow. For these families, the hope for a child isn't bound by age; it's a timeless ache, an unyielding desire that persists despite the passing years. It's a reminder of the resilience within these families, who, despite the pain and loss, continue to endure, hoping against hope that one day, their arms will be filled with the child they've yearned for, completing their family in ways words can never express.

I am reminded of situations when these words were said to young widows after the passing of their spouses or partners. Often, these words come from those close to them, trusted friends, or family members who, with good intentions, attempt to console the bereaved. Yet, amid their grief, these words can cut deep, for the void left by the departure of a soulmate is not easily filled, regardless of age.

Even if the passing occurred within the initial years of their marriage, something irreplaceable is lost. The love shared and the dreams woven together are bonds that cannot be fully comprehended by anyone else, especially when the departed is their soulmate. It's the person they envisioned spending the rest of their life with, the one with whom they planned a future. I'm reminded of my friend who lost her husband; their dreams were numerous. They had committed their lives to each other, envisioning a golden wedding anniversary, celebrations, and plans set aside for the future. Now, life has taken on a wholly different meaning for her.

Every day, she wakes up to an empty side of the bed, a tangible reminder of her loss. The routine they once shared is now a solo journey, and the void left behind seems unfillable. Despite the well-meaning suggestions from bystanders, the idea of moving forward without the love of her life feels like an impossible task. She strongly declares she will never love another or remarry, but those around her often believe it should be easy to start anew since she is, after all, still young.

However, the reality is far more complex. Age does not erase the depth of the connection, nor does it diminish the pain of loss. The grief of a young widow is not diluted by the passage of time; it lingers, aching and constant. Every cherished memory, every unspoken word, and every shared dream testifies to the love that once existed. Saying "You are still young" might imply the possibility of finding love again, but for the grieving heart, it often represents an impossible mountain of loss, a reminder that the future they pictured will never come to pass.

Death has cruelly snatched away the future they envisioned, where growing old together was a cherished dream. For many, grief becomes a relentless companion, a shadow that echoes the laughter, the love, and the plans that once filled their days. In the face of such loss, some find solace in choosing to honour their partner's memory through a steadfast commitment to love that transcends the boundaries of time.

The idea of moving on after the death of a beloved partner becomes a daunting prospect, especially for younger widows. It's not merely a matter of reluctance but a complex web of emotions, deeply rooted in the unique bond they shared. Unlike some, they choose not to remarry or pursue relationships, not out of fear or bitterness, but out of respect for the love they once had.

The heartache of losing a partner is not easily quantifiable by age. The depth of the connection, the shared dreams, and the intimate moments are not diminished because of youth. In fact, in younger widows, the pain often feels magnified. Their journey into life together was cut short, leaving a trail of unfulfilled promises and unrealised potential. As they navigate the aftermath of loss, the thought of starting anew can feel like a betrayal of the love they once shared.

Moreover, the fear of forgetting their partners often lingers. The idea of moving on can be misconstrued as a willingness to erase precious memories, replace shared dreams, or let go of the profound impact their partner had on their lives. The fear that a new relationship might blur the vivid details of their past love story can create internal conflict, making it difficult to contemplate the idea of opening their hearts to someone new.

For many younger widows, their choice to remain devoted to the memory of their partners is an affirmation of the enduring love that transcends the realms of life and death. It's a testament to the impact their partners had on their identity and the irreplaceable role they played in shaping their future. In their commitment to this enduring love, they find strength, purpose, and a way to navigate the world without the physical presence of their beloved.

In essence, the decision not to move on after the death of a loved one isn't a sign of stagnation; it's a choice to hold onto a love that has become immortal. It's a way of honouring the past while bravely stepping into an uncertain future, carrying the legacy of a love story that continues to shape their lives, and offering inspiration to others who witness their unwavering commitment.

Youthfulness doesn't serve as a shield against the prolonged ache of grief; instead, it can amplify the weight of loss. As the years trickle by, memories resurface—anniversaries, birthdays, and the echoes of unfulfilled plans and promises. These reminders aren't mere triggers; they're emotional time bombs that can plunge us into depths of sorrow.

There are mornings when the sunrise pierces through the curtains, and you awaken in solitude, tears trickling down, your heart heavy with the weight of unspoken sorrow. It's these moments when the loneliness feels consuming because the world seems unable to comprehend the depth of your pain. The thief called death has plundered the life you once envisaged a future intertwined, promising to grow old together now dissolved into wisps of longing.

My sister, my confidante—I envisioned a lifetime of shared laughter and stories, never imagining she would be the one departing prematurely. Her absence cuts deeper with each passing day, a constant reminder of the plans unfulfilled and the dreams left untouched.

And then, there's the vision of a mother's twilight years—a peaceful period where I anticipated assuming the role of caretaker, mirroring the care I offered my patients. But life, unforgiving and unpredictable, painted a different canvas. She departed at 53, a milestone age that was supposed to be a midpoint, leaving a void that cannot be filled.

The phrase "You're still young" in the wake of someone's passing carries a profound weight. It embodies the truth that the essence of those we love remains etched in our souls, defying the confines of mortality. It's a testament that their spirits, laughter, guidance, and love persist within us, woven into the fabric of our being. But it also encapsulates the reality that their physical absence is an irreplaceable loss—one that alters the trajectory of our lives, shattering the dreams of shared tomorrows. In navigating this journey of grief, the hardest lesson is learning to carry the memories without the presence—an opposition that embodies deep love and loss.

Grief isn't limited by age; it's a universal human experience. The loss of a loved one touches individuals across all stages of life, regardless of age or maturity. Whether young or old, the pain of losing someone dear is profound and significant.

As we journey through life, forming connections and relationships, each bond holds its unique depth and importance. When we face the departure of a loved one, the impact resonates deeply, regardless of our age.

Children and adolescents struggle with the loss of parents, siblings, or friends, navigating uncharted emotional territory. For them, grief can be especially challenging, as they attempt to comprehend and process complex emotions amidst their own developmental stages.

Adults, in the midst of their careers, relationships, and responsibilities, confront the loss of parents, partners, or mentors. The weight of grief isn't lighter merely because of life experience; it's an emotional upheaval that disrupts routines and challenges emotional resilience.

Even older people, though possibly more acquainted with the circle of life, experience the anguish of bidding farewell to lifelong companions, siblings, or friends. The passing of someone close brings forth a unique kind of pain that transcends the wisdom garnered over the years.

The depth of grief isn't measured by the number of years lived but by the depth of connection and love shared. Each person's grief is valid and carries its own weight. It's a testament to the enduring impact of relationships and the profoundness of human emotions—a universal thread that unites us all.

Toolkit of Meaningful Gestures

- **Listen with Compassion:** be present and listen attentively without judgement. Let them express their feelings, memories, and emotions without feeling rushed or dismissed.

- **Validate Emotions:** acknowledge their grief without diminishing its significance. Use phrases like, "Your feelings are completely valid," or "It's okay to feel this way."

- **Offer Practical Support:** help with daily tasks or offer practical assistance, like running errands, preparing meals, or helping with household chores.

- **Share Their Memories**: encourage storytelling or sharing memories of loved ones. Reflect on the positive impact they had and the memories that bring comfort.

- **Respect Their Process**: everyone grieves differently and at their own pace. Respect their need for solitude or company, understanding that grief unfolds uniquely for each person.

- **Provide Emotional Space:** offer comfort without imposing advice or trying to fix their feelings. Sometimes, silence or a gentle presence speaks volumes.

- **Sustain Support Over Time**: grief doesn't have a timeline. Continue offering support beyond the immediate aftermath, as the need for understanding and companionship might persist.

- **Offer Resources**: provide information about grief support groups, counselling services, or helpful literature if they express interest or need additional support.

POWERFUL CHAPTER TAKEAWAYS

1. The pain of losing a loved one isn't limited by age. Youthful individuals experience profound grief, facing the challenges of loss and mourning just as intensely as any other age group.

2. For young people, the loss of loved ones not only signifies the absence of their presence but also the shattered dreams and unfulfilled promises, intensifying the sorrow and emotional turmoil.

3. Even amidst friends and peers, grieving youth can feel isolated, navigating their grief while grappling with shared memories that amplify the sense of loss and the absence of a future they once envisioned.

CHAPTER 8

Don't Cry

I will not say: do not weep: for not all tears are evil.
— J. R. R. TOLKIEN

Crying is referred to as the act of shedding tears, mostly as a physiological response to strong emotions or physical discomfort. It is a natural and involuntary process in which tears, a combination of water, salts, and proteins, flow from the tear glands in the eyes and down the face. Crying is normally triggered by various emotions such as sadness, grief, happiness, frustration, pain, or relief, serving as a way for humans to express their feelings. In addition, crying can have physical and emotional benefits, including relieving stress and tension, seeking comfort and support from others, and processing intense emotions.

In relation to grieving, crying is one of the immediate and natural responses to hearing the news that a loved one has died.

Grievers should never be afraid of crying or feeling guilty or belittled for expressing their hurt and love through tears. They need to express their sadness by crying. So, we should allow them to be openly expressive and give them the reassurance we really care and understand what they are experiencing. Crying also provides an outlet for the suppressed emotions that can otherwise be detrimental to your mental and physical health.

When supporting those who are grieving, you can feel helpless as they cry uncontrollably. Your first thought may be to wipe their tears away and try to comfort them. However, it is important to know when to step aside and allow them to cry. This is necessary for the healing process due to the many benefits of crying. By allowing individuals the space and time to cry, it assures them you care about their feelings and emotions. On some occasions, you might even want to shed a tear or two as well. That's okay. You do not need to hide your tears. You must also express your emotions.

As I write these words, many continue to struggle with the difficulty of coping with and moving beyond the persistent ache and anguish of grief. We find ourselves struggling to navigate the tumultuous waves of emotion that accompany the loss of loved ones, whether it is a mother, father, son, daughter, or spouse. In some heartbreaking instances, multiple family members have been taken from us within days of each other, particularly during the past three and a half years, which I refer to as the "COVID-19 years."

Reflecting on the year 2020, life underwent unprecedented changes that no one could have anticipated. Families that once gathered and perhaps met daily were suddenly confined to living within their own isolated bubbles. Hospital visits were restricted, and traditional holiday gatherings, parties, and family outings were things of the past. Families couldn't even visit each other when they were unwell, and people were left to face their illnesses and even their passing alone.

The once-frequent visits to the hospital to bid a final farewell to loved ones were abruptly taken away. Church doors remained closed, and the customary funeral rituals were no longer permitted. Hearts were left broken and wounded, and the tears of love that should have been shed during final goodbyes were denied. The only solace for many was the release of tears. Every time they remembered their loved ones, tears would flow, offering a therapeutic release for their pain.

The scars and the pain of grief linger deep within our hearts for years, even after we've navigated through the storms. Flashbacks are a frequent occurrence, and the grieving process persists until we find the strength to coexist with the pain. Grief isn't something we completely heal from; rather, we learn to let it become a part of us, allowing it to grow around us like a vine. Our natural response to a wide spectrum of emotions, spanning from profound sadness, grief, and pain to extreme happiness and joy, often involves shedding tears.

It's frequently said that tears are a language our hearts understand. Crying is a healthy and natural way to release our pain. It provides a sense of comfort and soothing relief. When we express ourselves through tears, it's an innate response. Crying triggers the release of chemicals such as oxytocin, endorphins, and stress-relieving hormones. These chemicals, often referred to as "feel-good" hormones, not only help alleviate emotional pain but also offer physical relief.

After a good cry, there is a sense of calmness and mood enhancement that envelops us, leaving us feeling emotionally lighter and more at ease.

I vividly recall the days I received the heartbreaking news of my mother and sister's passing. It marked the beginning of a season filled with tears. Surprisingly, each time I allowed myself to cry, I felt a sense of relief. Strangely enough, the pain seemed to lessen as a result. This phenomenon can be attributed to the release of certain hormones during crying, indicating that there are indeed health benefits associated with shedding tears.

It is crucial to emphasise that crying is a perfectly natural response to grief and sadness. When people are mourning, they may feel the urge to cry for extended periods. Do not discourage them from doing so. Sadness often manifests in teary eyes, and at times, even in shouting and screaming. It's essential to give individuals the space and understanding to express their emotions as they navigate through their unique pain. They alone comprehend the depth of their sorrow and must be allowed to embrace and release their emotions as they see fit.

Advising those who grieve not to cry can lead to them suppressing, avoiding, or burying their genuine emotions, potentially causing long-term harm. Ironically, crying is often stigmatised as a sign of weakness, instead of a powerful means of healing. It serves as therapy for the soul. Due to the complex and challenging emotional process of grief, crying acts as a coping mechanism. It is how our bodies and minds cope with the shock and pain of loss and help us come to terms with the reality of the loss we have just suffered. It allows you to begin to process the emotions associated with grief.

It took the loss of my mother for me to truly grasp the significance of shedding tears. That comforting sensation that washes over you as a tear gently caressing your cheek is profound. As tears flowed down my face, I sensed a growing relaxation and a release of tension. It became evident that I needed to authentically embrace my emotions, allowing them to surface from deep within. To genuinely recover from grief, we must embrace the act of crying, as it is an essential part of the healing process.

We're likely all familiar with the saying, "Big boys don't cry" or "Big girls don't cry." Society often conditions us that it's not socially acceptable to shed tears after reaching a certain age. As children, crying was our means of expressing emotions, pain, and disappointment. Babies, without the words to articulate their hunger, sadness, or discomfort, communicate their needs through tears, which is perfectly normal. However, as we progress through life, crying gradually loses its role as a means of communication for our needs. Our parents might have attempted to console us by repeating the phrase "Big girls and boys don't cry" whenever we experienced disappointment or sadness.

Indeed, while society often accepts and even encourages females to be in touch with their emotional side, there persists a widespread perception that expressing grief is a sign of weakness, especially for men. This perception is influenced by a combination of social and cultural factors that foster the belief that crying is an indication of vulnerability. In this narrative, boys are held to a different standard, and to conform to their gender expectations, they are encouraged to "man up" and refrain from shedding tears. Consequently, their emotional experiences may be marginalised, and they may feel pressured to grow up quickly.

The message is clear: men are not supposed to cry, and this expectation leads many in our society to conceal their emotions. They often avoid embracing their true feelings for fear of jeopardising their perceived masculinity. This stereotype has endured for generations and persists in today's society, reinforcing the notion that if a man cries, he is weak.

Society has burdened men with the fear that their strength and masculinity are contingent upon their ability to maintain composure, holding back the tears that yearn to be set free. However, it's essential to understand that there are various reasons why some men don't cry at funerals. During my research for this book, I had the privilege of engaging in conversations with male friends and colleagues, and I encountered some unexpected yet relatable reasons, akin to what I personally experienced during my season of complex grief.

One individual I spoke with revealed that, in the midst of their grief, they were struggling with the profound challenge of accepting the harsh reality of what had just transpired. They were in a state of shock, striving to come to terms with their disbelief. In his own words, they described it as "wrapping my mind around it."

Another man shared that his reason for not crying was to demonstrate strength for those around him, including his wife, mother, sister, and children. He expressed a desire not to appear vulnerable, as people were looking up to him. He felt that others were forming judgements and opinions about him. Striking a balance was difficult because when he didn't display this perceived strength, he felt that the same people would later claim he didn't love the person or care enough.

He emphasised that people must understand those experiencing grief are still human beings with emotions. They feel and hurt just like anyone else. All they ask is for acknowledgment of their emotional experiences and the space to embrace and express those feelings.

It's essential to stop maintaining the feeling of invisibility that men experience during their grieving process. Men often struggle with loneliness when mourning as they frequently perceive that when visitors come to the home, they primarily direct their inquiries toward the female members of the family. One of my male friends stated that questions like, "How are you coping?" or "Are you okay?" are often posed to women, while men can feel overlooked.

Furthermore, they echo that men often find they don't receive adequate support from their own gender. When male friends or acquaintances visit, they might engage in conversations about topics like sports, the weather, or other casual subjects, almost as if there's a mental fog obscuring the significance of the loss. These conversations rarely centre around their feelings or the loss that has taken place days or weeks prior. As a result, men may feel that their male counterparts are less likely to engage in deep, meaningful discussions and may appear to have lost touch with their emotional side. It's crucial to change this dynamic and create a more supportive environment for men to express their grief and emotions.

My friend echoed this when he said he often felt unseen, carrying his grief like a hidden scar tattooed upon his heart. As he related his story to me, I could almost envision him and the pain that flooded his heart. I realise it took a lot of courage for him to share his worries with me. For the first time in years, I saw sadness envelope my friend's face. He continued by saying "It becomes a burden, not just for us but for those around us as well when we can't openly express our feelings to those we love, telling them honestly how we feel and the support that we need from them without the fear of being judged or categorised as less of a man.

The belief by society that real men don't cry leaves us to struggle to cope with the reality of this world." At that moment I realised I too had failed those precious souls in my life. I judge them unknowingly when they turn to alcohol to try and numb the pain, to stay hidden behind the wall of masculinity.

During our own season of grief, we fail the men in the family. We give them duties without realising they too are trying to figure out what just happened. At the funeral, we are protected, and their shoulders are readily available for us to lean on.

Oh, how wrong and blind I was. It took a conversation with my friend to understand the depth of uncertain emotion the passing of a loved one has on a man. Hence, it's essential to acknowledge that men, too, have tears, and at times, they need to feel them trickle down their cheeks. We need to give them silent moments to embrace and make sense of the reality around them. Society must move away from the rigid expectation that men should always be the unwavering pillars of strength, carrying the weight of the world on their shoulders while disregarding the emotions we hold within.

When it comes to grieving, there is no specific face or gender for sorrow. Most people shed tears when they lose someone close to them. There should be no fear associated with our tears. I understand that it can be challenging to support or know how to support those who are expected to be strong. Excessive expectations are placed upon a particular gender.

To provide meaningful support, try spending quality time with the person who is grieving without neglecting their holistic needs. Addressing their spiritual, physical, psychological, and emotional needs is crucial for effective support. In many cases, men may resort to unhealthy coping mechanisms such as alcohol or drugs to mask their feelings, emphasising the need for compassionate and comprehensive support during times of grief.

An online article entitled "Men and Grief: Understanding and Supporting a grieving man" reveals that 80 percent of men feel alone during their grief whilst 52 percent turn to alcohol or drugs as a means to cope with grief. On average, they consume alcohol 13 times more frequently each month, and 24 percent use recreational drugs daily during their grieving process. While these substances may offer temporary relief, their long-term effects can be devastating. Studies have shown that only 13 percent of men return to normal patterns of alcohol and drug usage after experiencing a loss, and in 30 percent of cases, these unhealthy coping mechanisms exacerbate their grief. 9

To effectively help and support the men in our lives, it's crucial to address their comprehensive needs. Let's demonstrate the support they require by involving them in meaningful conversations, checking in on their well-being, offering hugs, and being genuinely attentive listeners. I encourage you to create a space where they can freely express their emotions, whether it's through tears or words. Refrain from passing judgement on those expected to be strong, as even the strongest individuals can have moments of vulnerability. Encourage them to embrace their emotions.

If you are a man reading this, I urge you to allow yourself to feel. Experience every bit of pain that comes your way. Don't suppress your tears; let them flow and release the emotions within you. There are indeed therapeutic benefits to crying, and you will likely feel much better afterward. Seek support if needed, but remember, you don't have to go through it alone. Don't let anyone, whether friends or family, dissuade you from seeking therapy if it can help you make sense of a life-changing event and find peace. Your grief is a personal journey, and it's essential to navigate it in your own way, allowing yourself to be both the protector and the one who can be vulnerable with yourself.

It is important when supporting someone grieving that you allow or encourage them to cry if they have to. Remind them that it's okay to cry. There are several important psychological and emotional functions. They vary from person to person, depending on the duration of crying and grieving when someone dies. As grief is a complex and personal process, the duration of someone's grieving and crying for a loved one cannot be determined. Various factors such as the individual's relationship with the deceased, the circumstances of the death, and their coping mechanisms, all play a role.

It may take many months or even years to fully come to terms with the grieving process. Grief often includes various stages, such as denial, anger, bargaining, depression, and acceptance. Not everyone experiences these stages in the same way or order whilst others may not experience them at all. Some people may find that their intense grief lessens with time. However, others may continue to feel a deep sense of loss for an extended period.

It's essential to understand that grieving is a natural and necessary part of the healing process when someone close to you dies. There is no "right" or "wrong" timeline for grieving, and you should not feel pressured to conform to any specific expectations or timeframes. It's also crucial to seek support from friends, family, or professionals if you or someone you know is struggling with grief as it can be a challenging and emotionally draining experience. Ultimately, the duration of crying and grieving varies from person to person, and the most important thing is to allow oneself to grieve in a way that feels appropriate and healing.

As a healthcare worker who interacts with people from diverse cultural and faith backgrounds, it is important to understand and respect their beliefs and practices. This knowledge provides valuable insights into how to effectively support and care for patients and their immediate family members. It allows us to offer empathetic and culturally sensitive care, particularly in end-of-life situations.

By being aware of their cultural and religious practices, we can better comprehend their preferences and needs, which, in turn, enhances our ability to provide appropriate care and emotional support. This approach enables us to build trust, foster communication, and ensure that the care provided aligns with their cultural and spiritual values.

Eventually, this cultural competence enhances our capacity to provide compassionate and individualised care, facilitating a more positive healthcare experience for both patients and their families.

Religion and culture indeed play a significant role in shaping how we express grief, particularly when it comes to behaviours like crying in response to the death of a loved one. Various religious concepts and beliefs can influence people's reactions and attitudes toward mourning and grieving, including the act of crying. These beliefs often differ from one religious' tradition to another.

In most, if not all religions, mourning is considered a natural expression of sorrow and loss. Crying may be viewed as an acceptable way of releasing and processing emotions during this difficult time. It's seen as a normal human response to the pain of separation and is often encouraged as a way to find solace and healing.

Conversely, in other religious traditions, there may be different interpretations. Some individuals or religious communities might view excessive displays of grief, such as loud wailing or prolonged crying, as a sign of disrespect or a lack of faith. In these cases, there may be an emphasis on maintaining composure and demonstrating unwavering faith in the face of adversity.

It's important to recognise that within each religious tradition, there can be a spectrum of beliefs and practices. Not everyone within a particular religion will interpret or express grief in the same way. Additionally, cultural factors often intertwine with religious beliefs, further shaping how people respond to loss and express their grief.

We must understand and respect the diverse religious and cultural perspectives on grieving, including the role of crying. It can help healthcare workers, caregivers, and communities provide more empathetic and culturally sensitive support to those who are mourning the loss of a loved one. Let's take a look at some popular religions and how they view morning and crying.

Islamic mourning traditions encompass prayer, readings from the Qur'an, and periods of private contemplation and introspection on the benevolence of God and the fleeting nature of life. While grief, including tears and sorrow, is a natural response to the loss of a loved one, Muslims aim to convey their sorrow with restraint and dignity. Excessive expressions of grief, such as loud wailing or prolonged emotional outbursts, are discouraged, as they may be perceived as a challenge to one's faith.

Within various Christian denominations, expressing your grief by crying and mourning is widely regarded as a normal response to grief. The Bible itself recognises the act of mourning and offers words of comfort to those who find themselves in sorrow as found in Matthew 5:4, which reads, "Blessed are those who mourn, for they shall be comforted." Christian funeral ceremonies typically incorporate moments for introspection, prayer, and the open expression of emotions, including the shedding of tears. For Christians, the belief in the resurrection and the promise of eternal life serves as a source of solace and reassurance during times of mourning.

In Buddhism, the grieving process may differ across various Buddhist traditions. Although there isn't a particular focus on shedding tears, Buddhism promotes the recognition of life's impermanence and the certainty of death. As part of the mourning process, individuals may engage in meditation and reflection on the nature of suffering and the experience of loss.

Conversely, Hindu mourning practices can be shaped by regional and cultural variations. Crying is considered a natural and culturally accepted means of expressing grief. Traditional Hindu funerals encompass a series of rituals and prayers that aim to aid the soul's transition to the afterlife, and crying is an integral part of this comprehensive mourning process.

Within Judaism, mourning practices can exhibit variability across different branches of the faith. In the context of traditional Jewish mourning, referred to as "shivah," a notable emphasis is placed on seven days of mourning. During this time, family and friends frequently come together to provide condolences and support. The shedding of tears and the open expression of sorrow are both customary and fully accepted components of this mourning process.

Various religions across the world possess their distinct customs and beliefs concerning grief and the act of crying. These customs exhibit substantial diversity and can be influenced by factors including cultural norms and individual interpretations of religious doctrines.

It's crucial to recognise that even within a specific religious tradition, there can be considerable variation in how individuals and communities navigate grief and their emotional expressions,

WHEN SILENCE IS GOLDEN

including crying. Cultural influences and personal convictions further contribute to shaping mourning rituals and practices.

In all circumstances, it remains imperative to foster an understanding of and respect for these diverse cultural and religious perspectives. This understanding is essential when offering support and care to those who are grieving.

Being present and offering support to a friend or family member who is crying while mourning can indeed feel challenging. However, it's essential to recognise that your mere presence can be a meaningful and comforting gesture.

Remember that your role is not to stop them from crying but to provide a safe and nurturing space where they can openly express their emotions. By being there, offering a comforting hug, or simply holding them close, you convey your understanding of their pain and your willingness to share in their vulnerability.

Your presence signifies that you are a trusted and compassionate friend, someone they can rely on and confide in during this difficult time. Patience is key; allow them the time they need to heal and process their grief through crying. Your support, understanding, and patience will help them navigate their mourning journey with greater comfort.

Toolkit of Meaningful Gestures

- Active listening is a crucial form of support when loved ones are grieving. Give them your full attention when they wish to discuss their emotions or reminisce about the person they've lost.

- Resist the urge to interrupt or provide solutions unless they explicitly seek guidance or advice.

- Instead, focus on creating a safe space for them to express their thoughts and feelings without judgement.

- Validate their emotions by letting them know that it is okay to cry, feel sad, angry, or any other emotion they are experiencing at the moment.

- Be patient with them, there's no length of time or period in which they're expected to heal.

- Extend physical comfort through actions like offering a warm hug, holding their hands, or merely sitting closely with them. At times, these nonverbal gestures can convey your support and care more effectively than words. Your physical presence can provide solace and reassurance during their difficult moments of grief.

- Reminding someone of the benefits of crying during grief can be a supportive and reassuring approach.

- You can gently let them know that crying is a natural and healthy coping mechanism with several advantages such as emotional release, stress reduction, physical comfort, and healing.

By emphasising these positive aspects of crying, you can help your loved ones understand that their tears are a natural and beneficial response to their grief. It may offer them comfort and validation as they navigate through their mourning process.

POWERFUL CHAPTER TAKEAWAYS

1. Instead of telling people to stop crying, it's more helpful to offer support, empathy, and a listening ear. Acknowledge their feelings; validate their emotions and provide a comforting presence. Encouraging them to express themselves and offering to help if they need it creates a supportive environment that fosters emotional well-being and trust in relationships.

2. It can or may create a communication barrier. When people are asked to stop crying, they might feel judged or misunderstood, making it harder for them to open up or seek support in the future.

3. Suppressing emotions can lead to bottling up feelings, which can be harmful in the long run. It prevents the natural processing of emotions and can result in increased stress or mental health issues.

4. It dismisses or invalidates people's feelings. Crying is a natural and healthy emotional release. Asking those who grieve to stop can make them feel their emotions aren't valid or acceptable.

CHAPTER 9

You Lost So Many People—You Should Be Used to It

I'm not unhappy. I cry a lot because I miss people. They die and I can't stop them. They leave me and I love them more.
— **MAURICE SENDAK**

In the journey of grief, some carry the weight of not one, but many losses, each accompanied by a vast amount of pain, demonstrating the complexity of mourning. Yet, in the face of multiple losses, there often lingers an unspoken expectation: the notion that one should become accustomed to sorrow.

As someone who has weathered the storm of numerous departures, I know the burden is multifaceted. Each loss bears its own scars, etching memories, and emotions into the very fabric of our being. But what happens when the world whispers, "You should be used to it by now"?

In these moments, the innocent words of others can become the heaviest burden, casting shadows upon the genuine emotions of grieving hearts. The sentiment, however well-intended, rings hollow, minimising the depth of pain that accompanies each new absence. That I know too well. From June 2016 until this day, eight years and counting, my heart breaks over and over by the sorrowful hand of death in the personal light.

Though my journey may have started much earlier as a healthcare professional, I experienced death in a much different light when it reached the door of my heart.

As a nurse and a military veteran, I am no stranger to people dying. As a matter of fact, that is part of our daily routine in the hospital. Patients die and sometimes more than one each day. Yet, we carry on like nothing happened, and it is normal. Sure, one will argue that death is indeed a natural part of life.

When something happens on the job, we often don't have time to process or fully understand its impact. We may have the belief that it shouldn't affect us personally and that we should always maintain professionalism.

In healthcare, there's a belief we should remain stoic in the face of death as if it's just another part of the job. But the truth is, when we lose someone, whether at work or in our personal lives, it's never just a professional experience. The idea of distancing ourselves emotionally doesn't always work because we're human.

Sure, we're trained to handle tough situations, but that doesn't mean we're untouched by them. Every loss leaves a mark.

We might wear our professional hats, but that doesn't shield us from the impact of someone's passing.

There's a difference between what's expected of us professionally and how we really feel inside. It's okay to have those feelings, even if it seems like we're supposed to keep them separate. Acknowledging both our professional duties and our personal emotions is what makes us truly compassionate caregivers.

Many times, I witness families with tears in their eyes, and I feel the tears welling up in the corners of my own eyes. I quickly blink them away. The breaking point for me on the job came with the COVID-19 pandemic. The death toll was overwhelming. Death was happening too frequently, and I recall the exhaustion of going through the motions. I distinctly remember my colleague and me discussing the unfairness of death.

We were no longer simply performing our jobs; we were now feeling the impact of death and its presence all around us. We had never become accustomed to it; all those years, we built a wall to fulfil our duties. My heart had already tasted the bitterness of death four years prior. Now, I was experiencing the rawness of my struggle while trying to carry out my job, as my beloved mother passed away during the COVID-19 pandemic.

In June 2016, my feelings about death and loss got all mixed up. I'd felt this kind of emotion before, but this time was different. I lost my sister.

You see, dealing with loss is tricky. You might think there's a right or wrong way to handle it, but the truth is, it's different for everyone. Each person you lose is like a unique puzzle piece, and your heart reacts in its own way each time. It tries to fit each piece back together to create a perfect shape or image.

My sister's death started a kind of love-hate relationship with grief in my life. Before her, I'd lost people I cared about, but this hit differently. It felt like there was no rulebook for how to feel or what to do.

As I tried to make sense of it all, I realised that grief doesn't fit everyone the same way. There's no set path to follow, no right or wrong way to go through it. It's more like a rollercoaster with ups, downs, and unexpected turns.

Do you remember those stages people talk about when it comes to grief? Well, they're like a roadmap, but not everyone's journey looks the same. My sister's death showed me that the stages don't tell the whole story. The stage becomes very confusing as there is no correct order or pattern to grief. The harsh reality is that I was trying to navigate my grief using this stage. But I realised I was farther from them than I imagined. They did not work for me. I had to find my own way to navigate that grief. Until this point in time, I have come to realise that acceptance does not truly exist. We simply learn to navigate through the process of grieving.

What I've learned is that grief is a part of life, and it's okay for it to stick around. It's like a friend who hangs out with you, sometimes quietly and other times making a lot of noise. I found comfort in thinking of it as something that grows with me, kind of like a plant that never stops growing.

Years have passed, but my feelings about my sister's death are still here. Some days are tough, like a storm inside me, and other days, it's more like a soft breeze, bringing back sweet memories.

This journey through grief has taught me that it's okay not to have all the answers. It's okay for things to feel messy and mixed up. Grief is always there, shaping my life story in ways I couldn't have imagined.

So, my love-hate relationship with grief continues, a reminder of the love I had for my sister and the impact she made on my life. And as I move forward, I carry those memories with me, adding to the story of who I am.

In March 2020, something happened that I never saw coming. My mom passed away. You might think that, having gone through loss before, I'd be a bit more prepared for it. But let me tell you, it hit me like a ton of bricks, and I felt I was back at square one.

When my sister passed away, it shattered my world. The pain was immense, the void she left behind indescribable. But when Mom followed, the weight of loss was staggering. It was like the words to articulate my emotions escaped me, lost in the overwhelming flood of grief. My heart had shattered again and what was left got broken again. I know my heart will never be whole again because each time someone you love dies; it keeps hitting the same unhealed wound.

Surrounded by well-meaning individuals, their intentions to comfort often came with misguided expectations. As a nurse and a military veteran, the assumption was that I should be accustomed to loss and that death was a routine part of my life. What they didn't realise was that no amount of professional exposure prepares you for the personal devastation of losing loved ones.

The heartache was compounded by the circumstances: Mom's passing at the heart of the COVID-19 pandemic. The daily troll of death became a harsh reality, a stark contrast to the usual rhythms of life. It wasn't just statistics or numbers;

it was the personal loss of precious lives, including my own dear mother.

Through these experiences, I've learned that professional exposure to loss doesn't diminish the personal impact. Grief doesn't discriminate; it permeates our lives, leaving an indelible mark that no amount of professional detachment can erase.

The truth is that even those familiar with death's presence are not immune to its heart-wrenching effects. It's a story of navigating personal loss amidst professional responsibilities, a reminder that grief transcends professional boundaries.

Meet Ailmrej, a compassionate nurse who has dedicated herself to caring for end-of-life patients within the hospital's palliative care unit. Her role extends beyond medical care; she stands by patients and their families during their most vulnerable moments. Witnessing death or being present as patients breathe their last breath has become a part of her reality, a facet of her profession she embraces with grace and empathy.

Yet, amidst the hustle of a routine shift, an unforeseen and heart-wrenching event unfolded. Ailmrej's world shattered when a call pierced through the hospital's chaos; a patient was on the way, requiring urgent care. As the medical team hurriedly initiated CPR, wheeling the patient into the emergency department, Ailmrej's world froze. The patient fighting for life on the gurney was none other than her father.

Tragically, despite the frantic efforts, her father did not survive. In that agonising moment, amidst the flurry of medical urgency, a colleague's insensitive comment cut deep. The coworker said that Ailmrej should be accustomed to such losses, given her constant exposure to end-of-life situations. The callousness of those words struck her like a dagger, causing a surge of anger and disbelief. The person lying on the stretcher was not just a patient; He was her beloved father.

Adding to her unfathomable grief, Ailmrej had recently returned to work after experiencing the heartbreak of a stillborn baby. The insensitivity of the remark amplified her pain, leaving her feeling utterly lost and wounded. How could someone, a colleague no less, be so oblivious to the depth of her loss? In that poignant moment, the layers of professional detachment crumbled, revealing a grieving daughter mourning the loss of her father.

Ailmrej's story is a testament to the complexity of grief, transcending professional boundaries. It underscores the profound impact of insensitivity during moments of immense personal tragedy, reminding us all of the fragile threads that connect our professional and personal lives. There's no getting used to grief no matter how often you experience it. It doesn't come with a manual, and it doesn't get easier just because it's not the first time.

Grief doesn't follow a schedule, and it certainly doesn't care if you've been through it before or about your profession. It's not like a school subject where you can say, "Well, I've aced this test, so I should be fine the next time." No, grief doesn't work that way. It's messy and confusing, and each time feels like the first time.

It's tough when people try to comfort you by saying you should be used to it by now because it is not your first time. They might mean well, but grief isn't something you just get over. It's not a switch you can flip off and on. It's more like a constant companion, sometimes quiet and other times making its presence known.

So, I want to make it crystal clear: there's no getting used to grief, and there's no getting over it. Each loss is a new journey, and it hits differently every time. The pain doesn't diminish just because it's not the first time around. It's okay not to have it all figured out, and it's okay to still feel the weight of grief, no matter how many times you've walked this path.

For those supporting us during our time of mourning please know that in our world, loss has struck. It is a force that feels unnatural and out of order. It shakes the foundations of our sense of safety. During these moments, you might find yourself unsure of what to say or do, afraid that your words might unravel our emotions. But know this, all these uncertainties are part of the intricate dance we're learning with grief.

Our loved ones are not forgotten. In fact, the loss we carry resides just beneath the surface of every emotion, even those wrapped in happiness. We'd rather face the pain by hearing their names and remembering our loved ones than shield ourselves from the truth and live in denial.

Grief, in its intensity, is the pendulum swing of love. It's a sacred rhythm where the strength and depth of our love create waves of sorrow on the other side. Consider it an opportunity, a chance to stand together, shoulder to shoulder, with those who have faced one of life's most daunting challenges. Rise up with us.

The unexpected loss of a child, parent, or sibling can shatter a person, leaving fragments that can't be pieced together. While we endeavour to move forward, our lives will never return to what they once were. We'll find our path, but it's an individual journey, one that requires patience and understanding. However, it is important to refrain from urging us to "move on" or suggest that time heals all wounds. By acknowledging our brokenness, your acceptance means more than trying to fix what cannot be mended.

As the years go on, some days cut deeper, when the void of our loved ones' absence feels almost unbearable. Birthdays are laden with bittersweet longing for celebrations we cannot share. And the anniversary of their departure brings waves of emotions—days of reflection and melancholy. Approach these days with gentle understanding, for they are moments we need to navigate in our own way and time.

Witness our struggles. Stand with us during moments of celebration mingled with sorrow. Understand that even amidst happiness, grief is an unwelcome companion, a reminder of our irreplaceable loss.

In this journey through grief, may we find solace in the collective strength that arises from standing together. Let's navigate this journey together and recognise that it is in the embrace of both that we truly rise.

During the festive season, my heart feels heavier, for their places at the table remain empty, and the emptiness left by their absence echoes louder. Each missed soul occupies a unique space in our hearts, making it agonisingly hard to accept their absence.

It's in honouring their memories and acknowledging their absence that we carry their essence forward, embracing the love they left behind.

In the journey of life, there are some things we never get used to. Certain experiences like betrayal or the end of relationships recur; yet, they never lose their ability to deeply affect us. Despite encountering these situations repeatedly, they retain their power to cause hurt and pain each time they unfold.

Take, for instance, the pain of betrayal. No matter how many times we experience it, the feeling of trust being broken by someone we are close to remains a deep wound. The pain of betrayal resurfaces, leaving a lasting impact on our hearts, regardless of previous instances.

Similarly, the end of relationships, whether romantic or platonic, doesn't diminish in its emotional impact over time. Each time a connection fractures, the heartache and sense of loss are as touching as if it were the first experience of such pain. The familiar ache may even intensify. It reminds us that certain aspects of life, much like death, elude our attempts to become desensitised to their effects. They persist as potent sources of emotion, each instance carrying its weight of hurt and sorrow, regardless of familiarity.

In acknowledging this truth, we embrace the complexity of human emotions, understanding that certain experiences retain their ability to impact us deeply, no matter how many times we've traversed similar paths. The depth and resilience of our emotional landscapes are truly remarkable. Every experience of hurt or loss requires its own time for healing, regardless of how familiar we may be with such pain.

Recently, I met Jenny at an event, and our conversation veered toward the complexities of life. During this exchange, Jenny shared a personal experience that resonated deeply with the theme of navigating loss and the inability to grow accustomed to its weight.

While struggling to conceive, Jenny and her husband embarked on a challenging journey of multiple rounds of IVF. Despite the hurdles, their persistence paid off; their third round was successful. However, the joy of this success was tarnished by an unexpected source: her sister-in-law's response. Upon hearing the news, instead of celebrating this triumph, Jenny was met with a comment that cut straight through her heart. Her sister-in-law said that she should be used to the difficulties by now.

This seemingly innocuous comment had a profound impact on Jenny's emotional landscape. It wasn't just about the insensitivity of the remark; it highlighted a deeper truth that some experiences, like the longing for a family or the pain of infertility, defy any attempt to become accustomed to their weight. It mirrored the broader concept that certain life events, including loss and grief, hold an enduring emotional impact that resists familiarity.

Jenny's story reminds us that there are aspects of life, like the desire for a child or the pain of losing a loved one, which cannot be simply shrugged off or gotten used to, no matter how frequently they occur. The remark echoed the misconception that repeated exposure to certain struggles should lessen their emotional impact, an assumption that overlooks the perpetual weight of these experiences.

This story underscores the necessity for empathy, understanding, and thoughtful communication, especially in moments when our words might unknowingly add to someone's emotional burden.

As this chapter closes, it's important to acknowledge a widespread misconception not limited to healthcare professionals but experienced by anyone facing loss: the belief that repeated encounters with death somehow lessen its impact or make the grieving process easier. It suggests that because we've faced loss before, we should be accustomed to it, almost immune to its emotional toll.

Yet, the truth is far from this assumption. Each loss, whether it occurs within the realms of our professional lives or strikes close to our personal circles is unique and very impactful. It's a mistake to assume that familiarity with loss diminishes its weight or eases the burden of grief. In reality, the heartache and emotional upheaval that accompany loss are as intense as ever, regardless of past experiences.

This misconception isn't just unhelpful but also downright disheartening. When people are grieving, being told they should be used to loss by now only adds a layer of misunderstanding and invalidation to their pain. It overlooks the depth of their emotions and the individuality of their grief journey.

Therefore, we must debunk this myth and understand that grief doesn't adhere to a scale of familiarity. Each loss brings its own set of emotions and challenges. Instead of assuming familiarity breeds comfort, it's important to approach those who are grieving with empathy, compassion, and understanding. It's in honouring and acknowledging the uniqueness of each individual's grief that we offer true comfort and support.

Each loved one leaves behind a unique board of memories, woven into the fabric of our lives, and as individual as the paths we tread through grief. There's no handbook for becoming accustomed to grief. It's not a journey we grow accustomed to or master. Grief doesn't abide by a set schedule or follow a predictable pattern. It disappears and flows, taking on its own rhythm in each person's heart.

At times, grief seems to pause, creating a deceptive notion that the pain has subsided. But the truth is, the ache lingers persistently, an unwelcome companion that refuses to dissipate. The tears might dwindle; the sobs might quiet, but this silence doesn't signify the absence of pain. It's merely the heart's way of finding a temporary refuge from overwhelming emotions.

There are days when tears do not fall, and the visible signs of grief appear to be inactive. However, deep inside, the heart reverberates with the memories of those who have passed away. Their absence, laughter, and warmth leave an enduring presence that not even silence can eliminate. Grief is not limited to tearful faces; it is ingrained in the depths of the soul.

These moments of respite, where tears cease, don't signal the end of grief. Rather, they punctuate the ongoing journey through the maze of loss. They're brief interludes in the symphony of sorrow, moments where the heart takes a breath before diving once more into the depths of remembrance and longing.

In navigating the complexities of grief, it's essential to acknowledge that its essence isn't solely manifested in tears. It resides in the quiet moments, in the unspoken conversations, and in the persistent ache of missing those who've departed. This journey through grief shows the enduring love and impact of those we've lost—a journey that's far from linear and one that cannot be quantified by the absence or presence of tears alone.

The relentless departure of our loved ones, especially when it occurs in succession, creates a narrative that seems almost surreal to the outside world. It's a narrative that defies the conventional expectations of life's natural course, prompting questions about the nature of these deaths. Are they an inevitable part of life's cycle, or do they harbour a deeper, perhaps unsettling reality?

In the face of such continuous loss, the idea of "getting used to it" becomes a difficult concept to grasp. The sheer frequency of goodbye challenges the very nature of becoming familiar with grief. It's not about adapting to loss, but rather an ongoing interaction with sorrow that follows its own unpredictable path.

The external gaze, curious and sometimes well-intentioned, raises questions about the nature of these departures. Friends, family, and even acquaintances may attempt to make sense of the inexplicable chain of losses, struggling with their own discomfort in the face of such a series of tragedies. In response, the internal dialogue becomes a contemplation of whether the acceptance of this relentless grief is a genuine internalisation or a societal expectation.

The external world may pose the question, "Do we get used to it?" as an attempt to understand and perhaps comfort. Yet, the truth is, we don't get used to it in the traditional sense. It's not about adapting to the pain but learning to coexist with a persistent ache. The coping mechanisms become a delicate balance between the internal tumult and the external expectations placed upon us.

So, is it about getting used to it or living because of society's expectations? The journey through multiple losses challenges societal norms, inviting introspection into the nature of grief and the complex interplay between personal experience and external expectations. It's a journey that acknowledges the impact of each departed loved one, resisting the notion that familiarity with grief diminishes its depth.

Toolkit of Meaningful Gestures

- Offer your presence and a listening ear. Allow the bereaved to express their feelings without feeling rushed or judged. Sometimes, the most profound support comes from being present and truly listening.

- Grieving isn't a linear process; it ebbs and flows. Respect their pace and understand that healing takes time. Be patient and offer your support consistently, even when their emotions seem unpredictable.

- Assist with daily tasks or errands. Practical support like cooking a meal, running errands, or providing childcare, can alleviate some of the burdens during a difficult time.

- Choose your words thoughtfully. Offer reassurance and avoid clichés like "Everything happens for a reason." Instead, say, "I'm here for you," or "I'm so sorry for your loss."

- Understand that everyone copes differently. Respect people's need for solitude or time alone if they're not ready to engage or talk about their loss.

- Mark anniversaries or significant dates related to their loss. A simple message or gesture on these days can show you're thinking of them.

- Encourage professional support. Suggest seeking professional help if they're struggling with overwhelming emotions or finding it hard to cope. Support groups or counselling can provide valuable assistance during the grieving process.

- Remember, offering grief support is about being present, understanding, and compassionate. It's not about fixing people's pain but rather walking alongside them through their journey of healing.

POWERFUL CHAPTER TAKEAWAYS

1. Loss doesn't come with a handbook, nor does it follow a predictable path. Assuming someone should be accustomed to grief because of past experiences only adds to their burden. Whether in healthcare or personal life, each loss is deeply felt and uniquely impactful. Real comfort comes from acknowledging the individuality of grief, offering empathy, and understanding, rather than assuming familiarity lessens the pain.

2. Loss doesn't discriminate based on past experiences. Assuming someone should be accustomed to grief disregards the depth of emotions felt with each unique loss.

3. Every loss, whether in professional settings or personal life, carries its own weight. Each person's grief journey is unique and shouldn't be minimised by assumptions of familiarity.

4. Comfort and support for those grieving stem from empathy and understanding, not from assuming that repeated loss should make one immune to its impact. True solace is found in acknowledging and honouring the individual's emotions in their grief journey.

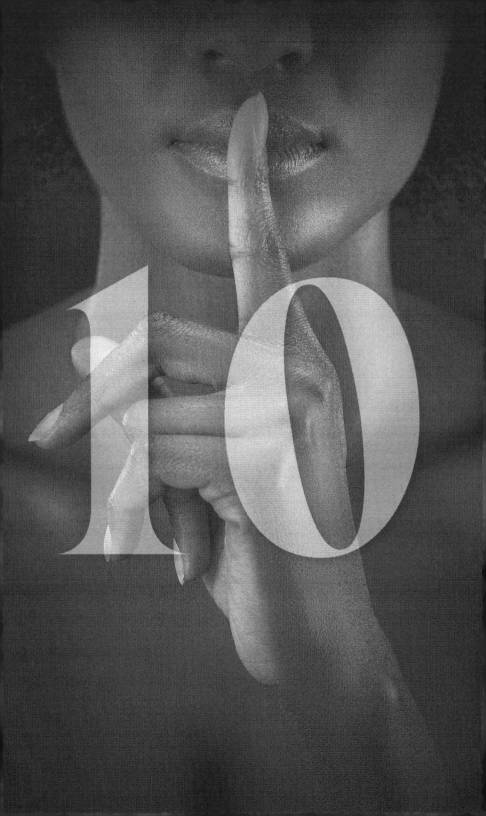

CHAPTER 10

It Happened for a Reason

Everything happens for a reason, but sometimes that reason is to simply teach us how to endure.
— **UNKNOWN**

I n moments of heartache and loss, we often encounter the phrase "Everything happens for a reason." It's a well-intended sentiment, a belief that seeks to bring meaning and purpose to life's most challenging experiences. Yet, as I've walked alongside individuals navigating the depths of grief, I've come to realise the limitations of these words.

Grief, with its profound and intricate layers, defies simple explanations or neatly tied reasons. It's a tumultuous journey marked by pain, confusion, and an enduring ache that reverberates through the soul. In these moments of profound despair, the notion that everything unfolds as part of some predetermined plan often falls short, unable to offer the solace it intends.

This final chapter explores the complexities of grief and the inadequacy of the saying, "Everything happens for a reason" in comforting those who grapple with loss. It delves into the raw emotions, the shattered dreams, and the sheer magnitude of sorrow that render such clichés insufficient in their attempt to soothe the inconsolable.

In our lives, one of the most inevitable truths is the reality of death. We all traverse this world with an understanding that we will someday bid farewell to those we hold dear. Yet, despite this universal certainty, conversations around death and dying often remain shrouded in discomfort and veiled by generic condolences, as if personalised discussions about loss seem too daunting to undertake.

Speaking to someone who is grieving is undoubtedly one of the most challenging conversations to engage in, especially when the right words escape us, leaving us with clichés and phrases that, upon reflection, feel hollow and insufficient. Families, unprepared for the harsh reality of death, often seek solace in these overused lines, only to realise later how painfully inadequate they are in the face of grief.

Growing up, I was accustomed to hearing, "It happened for a reason" or "It's for the best." While death is an inherent part of life's cycle, it leaves behind a gaping wound of inexplicable pain. Why we always try to find a reason for someone's death has always eluded me. I vividly recall a young man in our community whose departure prompted these familiar expressions.

He was often labelled as the most problematic individual in our neighbourhood. His life wasn't perfect, and people deemed him a source of trouble and shame for his family. However, amid these descriptions, there existed a different narrative: a portrait of a young soul with kindness embedded within. He was known to many as a loving boy, but his inability to steer clear of trouble overshadowed these traits. To me, he was a symbol of carefree living, someone unafraid to embrace life's risky adventures, regardless of the consequences.

He could hardly go by twenty-four hours without being involved in the wrong crowd at the wrong place at the wrong time. People often said, "Trouble follows that boy." However, his life was short-lived, and we never got to see what his future or older self would turn out to be, perhaps a lawyer, doctor, teacher, or even prime minister. Who knows? His adult life could have taken a different path from his childhood.

His passing was interpreted by some as a blessing, a relief from future troubles, a belief that his tormented soul found peace and his family was spared from anguish. Yet, for those who truly knew him, his departure was a stark reminder that behind societal judgements lay a person of depth, complexity, and an untamed spirit.

As I've grown older and experienced my own encounters with loss, I can't help but ponder the effects of death on the families left behind. The void and agony caused by death, while it might ease certain worries, also open an abyss of unanswered questions about what could have been. Regardless of how people live, death leaves behind enduring scars. Our loved ones are irreplaceable.

Many of the sayings passed down through generations, prove to be more destructive than comforting. The calamity lies in the fact that, instead of acknowledging and embracing grief, we replace it with advice, platitudes, and absence, failing to be truly present in our own moment of need.

While there's a common belief that beauty emerges from adversity, shaping our future, when it comes to loss and grief, that narrative often falls short. These moments aren't always transformative; they can be the most agonising and challenging times, where the overwhelming pain of grief takes hold. Understanding the reason and purpose behind the death of someone deeply loved seems an overwhelming task.

When my sister passed away at the young age of 23, leaving two children behind, I struggled with the saying that everything happens for a reason. I questioned the goodness in such a loss. In my grieving season, I found myself wrestling with faith, doubting God, whom I had trusted implicitly. My once solid relationship with Him was shaken. We used to talk every day, and I had unwavering faith in His provision.

Reflecting on my life journey, after leaving the army and diving into nursing school, I recognised instances where I felt God's presence. I got baptised during my nursing studies. Amidst the academic challenges, I felt blessed never failing an assignment and encountering unexpected provisions on my meagre student budget. Even as I supported my family in St. Lucia, God abundantly provided, defying what seemed impossible.

These instances of divine provision astounded me. But in the face of loss and pain, I struggled to reconcile the blessings with the tragedy of my sister's passing. It was a time when clichés and well-intended sayings fell short, leaving me struggling with the mystery of grief and faith.

I found myself in a place I never imagined, questioning the existence of God. It felt as though the God I once believed in was unjust and unfair. How could a loving God allow children to be left motherless? How could my sister, with dreams yet to be lived and children to nurture, be abruptly taken from our lives? The lack of closure, the absence of goodbyes or the chance to mend any wrongs weighed heavily on my heart.

As deaths continued to cascade through my family for six years, the strain on my relationship with God grew. It felt irreparable. Then, in 2020, when my mother passed away, it was as if God had abandoned me entirely. Losing her meant losing my foundational support, the linchpin of my family.

I struggled with the injustice of it all. It seemed unfathomable that a divine God, if there was one, would allow such heartache and pain to perpetuate, leaving us shattered and struggling to make sense of the unexplainable losses.

The absence of answers and the relentless succession of tragedies shattered my faith. It pushed me to the brink, leaving me with a sense of abandonment and disillusionment. In those moments of grief, God felt absent, distant, and unresponsive, leaving me adrift in an ocean of despair and unanswered questions. Yet, after each loss of family members, people kept saying, "It happened for a reason." I have grown to dislike this phrase.

Navigating grief, especially when it stems from inexplicable losses, seems to be a prevalent struggle on social media. Many individuals battle with the pain of losing loved ones because they cannot understand why it happened.

I vividly recall a devastating incident where an entire family perished in a tragic vehicular accident. They were on their way back from a funeral service when the bus they were travelling in veered off a cliff, resulting in a heart-wrenching loss; no one survived, not even the youngest, just a baby. Witnessing the aftermath at the funeral in Micoud remains etched in my memory: the sight of 14 caskets lined up under a tent, the anguished cries, the unrestrained tears. No explanation could alleviate that pain, nor could anyone assert a reason for such a tragedy.

That day, as I stood on the playing field, a place I knew so well, it seemed different. It was a site where I had triumphed, where I'd earned numerous medals and set track records that lingered in the memories of teachers and schoolmates. The track where I'd run countless races was now transformed, holding a different weight, a place where joyous memories clashed with the raw grief of those bidding farewell to their loved ones.

The echoes of my victories were drowned by the cries, tears, and heartache of families mourning their departed for the final time. Rows of caskets stood, each holding someone's beloved. They were not just names or faces but people cherished with every fibre of those present, individuals whose absence would leave an indelible mark in the lives of their loved ones. The spectators weren't cheering; instead, sorrow marked their faces as they lined up as far as the eye could see.

As I write, my thoughts drift to my time deployed in Iraq in April 2005 for six months, where soldiers lost their lives in the line of duty, fighting a war. Regardless of the justness or fairness of the cause, it was impossible to assert that our fallen comrades died for a reason.

These instances defy any attempt to rationalise or justify the loss. They exist as stark reminders of life's unpredictability and its capacity to deliver unfathomable heartache. No reasoning, no matter how well-intended, can reconcile the anguish borne from such tragedies.

While struggling with the profound losses and tragedies, the year 2020 brought a new wave of heartache: the COVID-19 pandemic. It was a time when heroes emerged, selflessly dedicating their lives to save others. However, tragically, amidst their valorous efforts, some of these heroes succumbed to the relentless grip of the virus.

Their deaths, as they fought tirelessly on the front lines, caused sombre reflection. Society often clings to the notion that everything happens for a reason. But how could one find reason or solace in the loss of those who laid down their lives while striving to protect and preserve others?

These heroes didn't meet their fate as part of some grand design or predetermined reason. Their sacrifice wasn't a cosmic exchange meant to balance scales. Instead, their deaths were an illustration of the immense toll exacted by an unforgiving pandemic, a stark reminder of the vulnerabilities and sacrifices of those who put themselves at risk for the greater good.

Their legacy isn't found in a reason for their passing but in the unwavering courage, selflessness, and dedication they exhibited in their final moments. They stood as beacons of hope and valour, their lives a testament to the extraordinary commitment to saving lives, even at the cost of their own.

We've all encountered these statements countless times, perhaps we have even spoken to them ourselves. But let me unequivocally say that if in the face of your tragedy, someone insinuates your pain was meant to happen, that it serves a purpose, or it's a steppingstone to your betterment, you have every right to distance yourself from such sentiments.

Grief is an excruciatingly raw experience, not confined solely to death. It infiltrates our lives when relationships fracture, when opportunities vanish, when dreams crumble, and when illness consumes us.

Allow me to reiterate the words I've spoken with unwavering sincerity. Certain aspects of life cannot be remedied. They cannot be fixed; they can only be endured. The lack of education regarding grief can cause the well-intentioned to make statements that do more harm than good. Breaking away from tradition is extremely challenging and embracing change takes time.

The statement "It happened for a reason" took on a different meaning in this context. It highlighted the struggle between societal perceptions and the complex reality of an individual's life. It emphasised the need to delve deeper and acknowledge the multifaceted nature of human existence, particularly in times of loss.

Death, often seen through the lens of finality, may also serve as a channel for deeper contemplation, a nudge to re-evaluate our understanding of life, the choices we make, and the complexities that shape each individual's journey.

The saying is often intended to provide comfort or offer a sense of meaning in the face of loss. However, its impact can vary significantly from person to person and situation to situation.

For some individuals, hearing those words might offer a sense of solace or a way to make sense of the incomprehensible. It might provide a glimmer of hope that there's a greater purpose or meaning behind their loved one's passing, helping them cope with the intense emotions of grief by framing the loss within a broader context. However, for many others, especially those in the midst of raw grief, this phrase can feel dismissive or even hurtful. It might come across as minimising the depth of their pain or implying that their loved one's death was somehow predetermined or necessary. This can be particularly challenging when the circumstances surrounding the death are tragic or seemingly senseless.

In reality, the complexity of grief often defies simple explanations or reasons. Attempting to rationalise loss with clichés can overlook the depth of someone's emotions or the uniqueness of their experiences.

What's essential when supporting those who are grieving is to be present, listen without judgement, and offer empathy and comfort without trying to explain away their pain. Validating their feelings and allowing them space to grieve in their own way can be more meaningful than trying to provide explanations that might not resonate with their experiences of loss.

When people are overwhelmed by grief, advice is the last thing they need. Their world has been shattered, making it a risk to invite anyone in. Trying to fix or rationalise their pain only intensifies their anguish.

I've witnessed the depths of sorrow and walked alongside individuals navigating their grief. I've come to understand the limitations of these words. They fall short in capturing the complexities of loss, failing to provide the comfort they aim to offer.

Grief, in its rawest form, defies simple explanations or reasons. It doesn't adhere to a script or conform to notions of cosmic balance. The tragedies we face, whether sudden and shattering or gradual and inevitable, defy any tidy explanations.

In sorrow, the assertion that "It happened for a reason" often feels inadequate, even callous. It disregards the immense pain, the shattered dreams, and the gaping void left behind. It overlooks the individuality of grief and imposes a narrative that attempts to rationalise the irrational.

Instead, what becomes profoundly impactful in these moments of despair is a simple yet powerful acknowledgment of the pain and the presence of those enduring it. It's the willingness to stand by others, to share their anguish, to listen without judgement, and to offer solace through presence rather than explanations.

As I reflect on the deeply personal and communal experiences of grief, I've come to recognise that while life's mysteries may never offer us clear reasons for our losses, the power of empathy, compassion, and silent solidarity holds unparalleled strength. It's in these moments of shared vulnerability that the true essence of healing and support emerges, transcending the need for reason and grounding itself in the human connection that sustains us through the darkest of times.

The most impactful action you can take is acknowledgment. Simply saying:

"I acknowledge your pain. I am here with you."

Notice I said, "with you," not "for you." "For" implies taking action, which isn't your role. Instead, your support and empathy hold tremendous power.

Acknowledgement requires no special skills or training. It's about being willing to be present with wounded souls, staying by their side for as long as needed.

Be there. Just be there. Don't leave when discomfort or feelings of helplessness arise. It's precisely in those uncomfortable, inactive moments that your presence matters most.

Healing often begins in those shadowy, seldom-explored places of horror. And it's within those spaces that having companions willing to join us is vital. Every grieving individual craves these supportive souls.

Therefore, I implore you; I urge you, to be one of these people. Your presence is more impactful than you can imagine. And when you find yourself in need of such companions, seek them out. I assure you; they exist.

Christmas is a season meant for joy and togetherness. It is a time that presents struggles for the many who will spend such a season without their loved ones. During these festive seasons, memories surge to the surface with an overwhelming force.

The first Christmas without loved ones is a formidable challenge, a journey of survival through a holiday season that once brimmed with laughter and shared moments. The attempt to wear a smile becomes a delicate art, a facade hiding the emotional tumult within. For some, it's a day marked by profound loneliness, where the echoes of joy that once filled the air are now overshadowed by grey skies and heavy hearts.

How does one ever grow accustomed to the absence of those dear to one's heart, especially when everything around triggers memories of shared celebrations? The decorations, the familiar scents, and the once-beloved traditions remind us of the emptiness. The "could haves," "should haves," and "would haves" linger in the air, creating a sad symphony of what once was.

In the midst of this holiday landscape, where others may perceive celebration, those who have experienced loss find themselves navigating through empty spaces. The notion that one should be accustomed to loss, having bid farewell to numerous souls, crumbles in the face of the enduring impact each departure leaves.

For those submerged in the depths of grief, being told it happened for a reason feels like an overview of an overwhelmingly complex reality. The idea that there's a hidden cosmic reason behind every tragic death makes it harder to feel the deep pain of losing someone important. It makes each person's life seem less unique and special, turning them into just a small part of a mysterious system.

The phrase may arise from a place of discomfort, an attempt to make sense of the inexplicable, or offer solace amid despair. However, its unintended consequence is to strip away the authenticity of grief, silencing the voices yearning to express the magnitude of their loss.

In the web of mourning, the attempt to rationalise death often creates a chasm between the griever's reality and the well-meaning intentions of those who seek to console. It fosters a disconnection, leaving the bereaved feeling unheard and misunderstood in their anguish.

The truth is that death doesn't always unfold according to a comprehensible narrative or a decipherable plan. It is often indiscriminate, leaving shattered fragments of lives in its wake.

To assert that it happens for a reason generalises the complexity of existence and the randomness of fate.

Instead of finding solace in scripted explanations, what grieving hearts truly seek is acknowledgement. They yearn for empathy, for a compassionate presence that doesn't attempt to rationalise or impose meaning but merely stands as a pillar of unwavering support.

The journey through grief isn't about finding reason within the inexplicable; it's about learning to carry the weight of loss and allowing the echoes of departed souls to resonate within us. It's about honouring their memory, their essence, and the profound impact they had on our lives, without seeking futile explanations for their departure.

Toolkit of Meaningful Gestures

- **Presence Not Words:** sometimes, being there without saying anything can offer the most comfort. Your physical presence communicates support and empathy more profoundly than any words.

- **Acts of Service:** offer practical help, such as cooking meals, running errands, or helping with household chores. These simple gestures ease the burden of everyday tasks during difficult times.

- **Listen and Validate:** create a safe space for them to express their feelings. Listen actively and without judgement. Validate their emotions by acknowledging the depth of their pain.

- **Memorializing Loved Ones:** help them honour the memories of their departed loved ones. This could involve creating a memorial, planting a tree, or organizing an event to celebrate their loved one's life.

- **Send a Thoughtful Note or Gift:** a handwritten note or a small, thoughtful gift can show you're thinking of them. It doesn't need to be elaborate; a heartfelt gesture speaks volumes.

- **Offer Time:** Be patient and give them time to grieve. Grief isn't a linear process, and everyone copes differently. Offer ongoing support without expecting a specific timeline for their healing.

- **Support Coping Mechanisms:** respect their ways of coping with grief, whether it's through art, exercise, journaling, or seeking therapy. Encourage healthy coping strategies.

- **Check-in Periodically:** grieving doesn't stop after the initial loss. Check-in on them periodically, especially on significant dates or during tough times, to remind them they're not alone.

- **Attend Support Groups Together:** offer to accompany them to grief support groups or therapy sessions if they're open to it. Your presence can provide reassurance.

- **Remember and Celebrate:** remember their loved one on special occasions or anniversaries. Acknowledge these days and, if appropriate, celebrate their life together.

POWERFUL CHAPTER TAKEAWAYS

1. Grief isn't a puzzle to be solved or a problem to fix with explanations. Authentic acknowledgement of someone's pain and loss holds more value than attempting to rationalise or find reasons for their grief.

2. Being there for someone in grief is about empathetic presence rather than imparting advice or clichéd phrases. Your support matters most in the form of compassionate listening and companionship.

3. Each person's journey through grief is deeply personal and unique. It's crucial to avoid comparing one's grief or assuming familiarity with loss based on past experiences, as each loss brings its own set of complexities and emotions.

Index

Here is a summary of some of the well-intended phrases covered in this book.

- "They're in a better place." While well-intentioned, this may not provide comfort as it minimises the griever's pain and doesn't address their immediate feelings of loss.

- "I know how you feel." Even if you've endured grief, each person's experience is unique. Saying this can make the grieving person feel unheard or invalidated.

- "You should be over it by now." Grief doesn't have a time-line, and suggesting someone should be done grieving can add pressure and invalidate their emotions.

- "It was meant to be." Implying that the loss was predestined or part of a grand plan can be dismissive of the pain and complexity of the situation.

- "At least they lived a long life." Length of life doesn't diminish the depth of grief. It's not about the duration but the impact of the loss.

- "You need to stay strong for others." Encouraging someone to suppress their emotions can be damaging. It's okay to feel and express grief.

- "You'll find someone else." Minimizing the significance of the relationship by suggesting easy replacement can be hurtful.

- "Everything happens for a reason." This phrase can feel dismissive and fail to acknowledge the depth of pain.

- "I understand how you feel; my pet passed away." Equating different types of loss may trivialise the person's grief over a human relationship.

- "It's time to move on." Grief isn't something to move on from but rather to navigate through, and suggesting closure can feel insensitive.

It's important to offer support, empathy, and a listening ear, rather than trying to offer explanations or minimise the grieving person's feelings.

Epilogue

As we draw the curtain on this journey through the nuanced landscape of grief and loss, we hope the words within these pages have resonated with you, providing solace, understanding, and a roadmap for healing.

In the quiet moments, amidst the weight of unspoken emotions, we find a profound truth—that sometimes, the most powerful messages are conveyed not through words but through the silence we share.

So, what lies ahead for me and my work and service in death, grief, and loss? It's time to speak to the needs of health-care professionals and other providers who deal with death constantly. I am speaking of:

- Doctors and Physicians
- Nurses
- Hospice and Palliative Care Workers
- Paramedics and Emergency Medical Technicians (EMTs)
- Funeral Directors
- Social Workers
- Psychologists and Counsellors

- Chaplains and Spiritual Care Providers
- Respiratory Therapists
- Firefighters
- Police Officers
- Coroners and Medical Examiners
- Military Medical Personnel
- Occupational Therapists and Physical Therapists
- End of Life Doulas

As a healthcare worker, I think that much is being ignored in how we deal with and process death since we are operating in "our jobs."

To address the need for self-care for health practitioners and other support agencies, I will work on my third book, *Nurturing the Healer from Within: Empowering Healthcare Heroes with Self-Care Strategies for Healing Amidst Loss*. This book will be a beacon of guidance, a practical guide crafted to empower you, the caregiver, with strategies for nurturing your mental health in the face of profound challenges.

Another project I will embark upon is the creation of "Soul Mend—A Self-Directed Grief Support Program" geared toward people who find it challenging to navigate life after loved ones die. This initiative is designed to be your companion on the path to healing, offering personalised resources and insights tailored to your unique journey.

The third thing I will work on is having a fully loaded website. This digital space will serve as a dynamic hub, offering various resources, community connections, and interactive tools to further assist you in your healing process. Visit and revisit, finding new insights and connecting with a community that understands the language of grief and healing.

Why am I doing all of this? Because the heart of the matter is that self-care is non-negotiable when dealing with death, grief, and loss.

Thank you for being on this journey with me as I heal and help others do the same. Cheers to more great things ahead.

With heartfelt gratitude and anticipation,

Jermila Sealys

Author of *Letting the Pain Out*

Acknowledgements

I'm overflowing with gratitude as I reflect on the journey of creating this book, and I wanted to take a moment to extend my heartfelt thanks to each and every one of you who made this possible.

To my extended family: your unwavering belief in me, your constant support, and the encouragement you've given me throughout this process mean more than words can express. Knowing you were behind me for a second round meant the world.

To my mentor: Dr. Nadine Collins, your guidance has been the compass that steered me through this intricate process. Your wisdom and insights have shaped this book in ways I couldn't have imagined. This book owes much of its existence to your invaluable mentorship.

I would also like to express my sincere gratitude to the dedicated editor who played a crucial role in refining and enhancing the narratives within this project. Your keen eye, thoughtful suggestions, and meticulous edits have been invaluable in shaping these stories into their final form. Your commitment to clarity, coherence, and emotional resonance has elevated the impact of these narratives, and I deeply appreciate the time and effort you invested in this collaborative process. Thank you for your expertise and unwavering support.

And to you, dear readers: as you turn the pages of this book, I hope my words become a comforting companion along your own journey through grief. May my experiences offer solace and encouragement as you navigate the twists and turns of this intricate path. Feel free to immerse yourself in the emotions within these pages. Let us walk together down that narrow street of grief—I'm extending a virtual hug to each one of you.

For those who are yet to join, I invite you into my community, where we can connect on various social media platforms. The writing in this book stems from my personal encounters with loss and grief, hoping it resonates deeply within your hearts.

Lastly, a special thank you to everyone who has purchased this book. Your support means everything to me.

With love and heartfelt thanks.

Jermila Sealys
Author, BSc, RN

Resources

Chapter 8

This chapter looks at the saying "Don't cry" while grieving. According to statistics, men find other methods of mourning rather than crying. It is reported that most turn to substance abuse.

Retrieved from "https://www.sueryder.org/grief-support/about-bereavement-and-grief/men-and-grief/"

Author Bio

J ermila Sealys holds a Bachelor of Science in Nursing with 10 years of experience working in the field. She is a British Army veteran who went on a mission to Iraq and is familiar with sudden death as a result of casualties on her job and also having a significant amount of sudden loss of close family members.

For the past 6 years, she has been the casualty of the sudden death of loved ones within close proximity of each other. After years of bottling up all her emotions and pain, she shares the courage to let the pain out and learn to release from grief and loss. She is ready to empower others to open up to the pain, tears, fears, and guilt of grief and loss to live everyday life.

She is passionate about working with women who have suffered the loss of loved ones unexpectedly. Her goal is to provide support to empower and educate women on aspects of death as a natural part of life and not as seen through taboo lenses. Through her transformation, she is now a Grief Support Coach, Speaker, and Author.

OTHER BOOK

'Letting the Pain Out' is me at my most vulnerable and powerless state. It reveals truths and lessons that I have endured during my over six years of silently battling grief at the sudden death and loss of loved ones. It is packed with stories of my struggle and how I finally managed grief without losing my mind. The silence and tireless tears that flooded the gates of my heart are finally now released. And as I share with you through the pages of this book, I continue to experience a form of healing and therapy.